GREATER THAN

THE POWER
AND STRENGTH
OF EMOTIONAL GRIT

JENNIFER FERNJACK

Greater Than: The Power and Strength of Emotional Grit ©
Copyright 2021 Jennifer Fernjack

First Edition
ISBN: 978-1-952976-27-8
Library of Congress Control Number: 2021915240

Cover Photo: Oliver Roos
Cover and interior design: Ann Aubitz

Published by Kirk House Publishers
1250 E 115th Street
Burnsville, MN 55337
Kirkhousepublishers.com
612-781-2815

GREATER THAN

Kirk House Publishers

DEDICATION

To my eye doctors who noted subtleties and
Acted on a hunch,
My surgeon, who had the knowledge of risks
And the wisdom to mitigate them,
My friends and family who provided
Unconditional love,
And a loving God who never let me
Walk alone in the sand...
I am forever grateful.
And to my parents with
Love and adoration
You don't just promote emotional grit,
You embody it.
I am who I am today because I learn
From you.
And to the people who provided
Real-life stories for this book,
Thank you for doing so, so that others may not only learn
from them
But feel inspired.
The best things in life...
Are free.

To Connie Anderson, Ann Aubitz, Brooke Dierkhising, Julie Finch, and the Minnetonka chapter of Women of Words (WOW), thank you for not only believing in this book but believing in me. I couldn't have finished this incredibly detailed project without you. Your insight and wisdom helped guide me through the process of writing, editing, design, and more. For that, I am truly grateful.

TABLE OF CONTENTS

CHAPTER 1
Infinite Possibilities

◆ ◆ ◆

"You never know how strong you are until being
strong is the only choice you have."
— Bob Marley

When experiencing the challenges that life has to offer, it is easy to take things at face value. The true value can be hidden, though, in plain sight. Yes, wins are wins, but losses can have benefits too. They reveal the importance of discipline and drive when honing your craft or realizing that you're capable of far more than you imagined when life has other plans—making it possible to persevere with the power and strength of emotional grit.

My personal story of grit stems from a surprising medical diagnosis I received in 2016. Knowing that I couldn't *not* experience it, I had to figure out the *how*. People would ask me how I got through the diagnosis itself, the anticipation of the dangerous surgery, and the corresponding emotions that came with it. It was then that I began to reflect on other people's stories of emotional grit so that I could try to understand my own.

For example, I thought about how when Cindy Crawford was growing up, kids would tease her because of the distinctive mole on her face. Feeling self-conscious and discouraged, she wanted to have it removed. Her mom convinced her otherwise, and rather than hold her back, the mole helped propel Cindy forward in an industry where she became known for her looks and was called a supermodel.

I also thought about "adaptive sailing," wherein visually impaired sailors compete in races without sighted crew members. They can do so by using buoys that emit the sounds of foghorns, whistles, or sirens. Audible devices are also put on the boats themselves so sailors can tell when another boat is near.

FAA Operations Manager Ben Sliney came to mind, too. After witnessing the horrors of 9/11, he knew that more planes could be hijacked, so he gave the unprecedented command for over four thousand planes in US airspace to land. How was he able to do this? He was the head of the FAA's command center in Herndon, Virginia. What was the catch? It was his first day on the job.

So, whether it is a result of times of uncertainty as an individual or moments of incredible stress on the job, it's interesting to note not just what we're capable of but also the physicality of how we're wired. While traveling for work, I would have amazing conversations with people about the intricacies of the brain. For example, we wondered:

- How is it that a man from Washington could become a math genius after suffering a brain injury from an attack outside a bar? (Acquired Savant Syndrome)
- Why can't some people feel pain and temperature? (Congenital Analgesia)
- Why do some people have a sudden change in speech after a stroke or traumatic brain injury, where they're now thought to be speaking with a foreign accent? (Foreign Accent Syndrome)

- Why doesn't my friend Stacie cry tears? (Potentially Lacrimo-auriculo-dento-digital Syndrome.)

The examples listed are incredibly rare, but they gave me pause as to how the brain has the ability to do more than we ever imagined.

As I began to research things that helped me feel less stressed during my medical scare, I wondered if there was science behind them. I asked questions such as, "Why does listening to my favorite music bring me joy? Why does it make me feel good if I do something nice for someone else? Why do genuine feelings of gratitude give me a sense of peace?" Imagine my surprise when I learned that music, acts of kindness, and gratitude can lower the stress hormone cortisol. The same can be said for laughter, pets, and facing your fears. They all also have the ability to influence the "feel-good" chemicals of the brain, such as: dopamine, serotonin, oxytocin, and endorphins. The key is to be open to things that can trigger them. I write that because even though I could benefit from a "runner's high," it's probably not going to happen because I don't want to run.

On the other hand, there are amazing stories of people who not only run marathons but do so under extraordinary conditions. When I was in college, I worked at Grandma's Saloon & Deli, a popular restaurant in the Canal Park neighborhood of Duluth, Minnesota. It is on the shores of Lake Superior at the base of Duluth's historic Aerial Lift Bridge that serves its shipping canal. Huge ships from around the world would enter the harbor with commodities such as iron ore, coal, or stone. As they did so, the bridge would rise to grant them entry. The ship and bridge operators would then greet each other with loud bells and horns that carried over the largest freshwater lake, by surface area, in the world.

Since 1977, Grandma's Saloon & Deli has sponsored a marathon that attracts thousands of people—including runners from all over the world. My first year on the job, I heard about people who had run the marathon the year before, even though it was only 39 degrees outside! I've also heard stories of people who run marathons even though they can't see. They can do so with the help of volunteers who serve as "guide runners." Different methods include "elbow lead," waist-to-waist, or hand-held tether and verbal cues. Yes, ability and opportunity are important, but being willing to do something can be half the battle.

Wanting to learn more about other stories of emotional grit, I began to reach out to people for this book. As I did so, I wondered how my friend Jesse could study for the Law School Admissions Test (LSAT), even though he is legally blind. I also thought about when my mom's friend Pam made the decision to give her kidney to her aunt and how my friend Dave rode his bike for an hour and a half both to and from school on the icy streets of Minnesota, even during blizzards, when he needed to take a class. (At the time, he wasn't able to drive due to what was thought to be a nitrogen embolism from serving as a pilot overseas.) These are all great examples of emotional grit. Through research and impactful introductions, I was able to learn about the grit it took for the college-age boys of the 1980 US Olympic hockey team to beat the mighty Soviets during the Cold War, as well as selfless efforts of first responders – Including those who served at Ground Zero on 9/11.

People often assume that being brave is the absence of fear, when in reality, bravery can be the act of feeling afraid and persevering anyway. Just months after my surgery, I was invited to get on stage at my church to share what had happened—and how I had been able to get through it. I was given just a few days' notice that I would be speaking at four different services for people who were there in-person, streaming the service from their homes, or watching the service overseas. Knowing that the sanctuary seated nearly one thousand people, my pastor asked if I would feel comfortable on stage. (I had done public speaking before, but for no more than sixty to seventy-five people at once.) It was possible that I could get nervous, but wanting to share my personal message of hope and grit with others, I knew that my decision couldn't be about me. That was when I had the epiphany about what I call "greater thans." (This can be illustrated with the pointer finger and thumb of the right hand to make the "greater than" symbol, like in math class.) Reason being that my desire to help others was "greater than" my fear of the stage. It didn't mean that I couldn't be afraid—it just meant that I was going to do it anyway. The concept can apply to anything in life, so as you read this book, please think of any "greater thans" that you may have. For example, as a parent, you may be going through a contentious divorce, so your love for your children needs to be greater than your disdain for your ex. Or perhaps you're a first responder whose sense of duty is greater than your sense of self. While stress can't always be eliminated, it's encouraging to know that there are ways to reduce it and persevere.

People ask me if I think a mindset of emotional grit is nature or nurture, meaning: are people born with it, or is it learned? While I can't speak to the potential genetics of it, I'm a firm believer that nurture played a huge role for me.

CHAPTER 2

Hidden Treasures

◆ ◆ ◆

"Learn from yesterday, live for today, and hope for tomorrow."
— Albert Einstein

I t's common for people to teach kids how to share, take turns, have good manners, and be responsible for putting away toys, but what we're taught as adolescents is important, too. These formative years can be influenced by the *way* we were raised, *when* we were raised, and *where* we were raised. Experiences from our youth can then be drawn upon when we're older.

I was raised by family, influenced by mentors, and offered opportunities to learn from others, including friends, neighbors, teachers, coaches, employers, coworkers, and even my old dermatologist. The experience of going away to college and being able to travel helped to forge my mindset of emotional grit as well. As a lifelong learner, I've realized that individual moments may not carry a lot of weight, but collectively, they can shape us. Plus, in addition to learning from your own mistakes, you can learn from the mistakes of others or follow their lead. I believe that the climate in which I was raised and the era I was born in played a role in my development because without the ability to use a smartphone or surf the internet, I had to make my own fun by playing in the snow—just like my peers.

Way and *When* I was raised

Family

Examples and lessons of emotional grit go back in my life as far as I can remember. The thought in my family was that even though they couldn't protect me from all of life's risks, they could still provide me with tools, rather than crutches, for dealing with them. As they did so, certain themes began to emerge:

> • *Life's challenges and limitations can make us stronger and wiser—when we learn from them.*

Through fifth grade, I was raised half a mile up the street from my grandparents, so I would frequently ride my bike there. On one such trip, I was pedaling my bike down a hill way too fast, so I wiped out when the tires hit loose gravel. After walking my bike home, my dad could hear me crying from the garage, so he came out to make sure I was okay. As he comforted me, he could see that I was just scared, not hurt. So, when I was done crying, he asked what I had learned from the experience. Rather than tell me that I couldn't ride fast again, he encouraged me to weigh the risks on my own. Yes, I could have fun by speeding down the hill again, but was the potential fall worth the risk? I had to make the decision for myself. In doing so, I could learn from it. After all, how could I learn from my mistakes if I wasn't allowed to make any? Sometimes the lesson is the blessing. This mindset also applied when I accidentally tossed my retainer, along with the garbage on my food tray, into one of my high school lunchroom's trash bins. My dad told me that if it happened again, he would pay for half, but the remaining half would come from either my allowance or babysitting money. After that, any new retainers would be on me. Now that I had skin in the game, I was more responsible with the next one rather than taking it for granted.

There's a difference between consequence and punishment. Consequence is the result of an action, whereas punishment is retribution for a wrongful act. Having an awareness of potential consequences helped me make decisions by sharpening my ability to weigh options and calculate risks. By being allowed to make individual mistakes and experience loss as an adolescent, I began to mature and handle the larger challenges that life had to offer.

• *Benefits can be where we least expect them.*

From a young age, my parents taught me to think through stuff, think outside the box, and think on my feet. I learned to improvise, asking questions such as, "What have I got, and how can I make it work to get me what I need?"

My friend Dayna and I loved playing with Barbie dolls. Between the two of us, we had a number to choose from, but we didn't have the coveted pink Barbie Corvette, so we improvised by having our Barbies "drive" slippers. We also had them "sleep" on Velveeta boxes and use Kleenex for "covers."

At the time, my friends and I weren't just given games to play—we had to create our own. If we happened to complain that we were bored, our parents would say, "Use your imagination." So, we learned to entertain ourselves. Initially, this took some effort, but then it became a habit and then a mindset. My friend Colette and I would make haunted houses for our siblings, my friend Denise and I pretended we were in plays for my mom, and my brother and I made forts with couch cushions, blankets, and dining room chairs. Dayna and I also played in the woods and made mud pies—thanks to her backyard and crab apple tree.

My friend Michelle was a Girl Scout, so at the age of eight or nine, she asked me to sell Girl Scout cookies with her. We did so by going door-to-door to the homes of neighbors between my house and my grandparents' house. By doing this, we learned how to market the cookies, collect and make change, and deliver the cookies on time. My friends Paul, Daryl, and Justin had similar experiences with paper routes and lawn mowing or shoveling businesses as kids.

Paul Engstrom's sign as an early teen

The thing about paper routes was that they could be early in the morning, often when it was still dark outside or freezing with snow. Regardless, people still wanted to read the news, check out the classifieds, and clip coupons. (Especially since reading the news online wasn't an option yet!) The people I mentioned started small and went on to develop some of the best work ethics I know.

My grandpa was a good influence. Rather than buy new nails, he would pound out bent ones so that he could reuse them. This mindset to "do the best with what you have" stemmed from his experience during the Great Depression. I couldn't fully appreciate where he was coming from, though, until I bought my first house in my mid-twenties. Money was tight, so I worked two jobs and rented out my spare bedroom to make my car payment. It was an older home, so when some cupboard doors became loose, I was afraid that I would need to *replace* them. Imagine my surprise when my grandpa brought over a box of matches with the idea of using them to *fix* the cupboards instead. He did so by breaking off the flammable ends of the matches and then using the remaining sticks to fill the holes beneath the metal hinges. Then he tightened the screws into them as a way to secure the doors. There was no need to incur the expense of new ones. I could just make the best of what I had and be grateful for it. While he was teaching me to fly, his wisdom also helped me stay grounded.

My hometown of Cloquet, Minnesota, has a paper mill where some of my friends' parents worked. During our college years, some of those friends paid for their college tuition by working at the mill as "vacation replacements" during summer breaks. Their roles were subject to split shifts, so they could be working during the day, evenings, or overnight. (Not necessarily ideal for college social life!) Years later, when I asked a couple of them independently of one another whether they were glad they had had the experience, neither hesitated to say yes. The reasons they cited included things such as learning to talk to adults, gaining a greater appreciation for the work their parents did, and having an incentive to take college seriously (as they knew paying for any additional classes may literally have had to come out of their paychecks).

• *It's possible to gain a greater appreciation for what you have when you have something to lose.*

When I was in college, it was common for people to use beer crates as coffee tables. People would put their feet on them when they were wearing dirty shoes, and no one seemed to worry about water rings from glasses. One friend in particular had such a "coffee table" and allowed people to put "spit cups" on it when they were using chewing tobacco. A few years after we graduated, I visited him at his new apartment. We had gone from sharing classes together to having full-time jobs, so I looked forward to hearing how he was doing. Knowing how relaxed he was about his stuff at school, I started to set my water glass down on his new store-bought coffee table. Imagine my surprise when he practically threw himself across the room to hand me a coaster for it. Turns out that he had paid for the furniture himself with his new job, so he had something to lose if it was damaged. To this day, we still laugh about what happened.

This relaxed mindset during our college years was also prevalent when landlords charged students a flat rate each month for rent and utilities instead of rent plus a percentage of the utilities, knowing they could fluctuate. I remember classmates who would purposely leave windows open because their rooms were too hot rather than turn down the heat—because either way, they paid the landlord the same amount each month. Of course, they may have felt differently if they had had to share the cost of the increased heat bill!

• *It's possible to appreciate things more when you earn them.*

As a math teacher, my dad tried to incorporate academic principles into everyday life so that I could learn from them. For instance, when I was in third grade and asked if I could get my ears pierced, he said I could do so if I memorized my times tables first. When I finally sat in the chair to have the piercings done, I felt a sense of achievement because I had "earned" the ability to do so through setting goals and the use of my flashcards. (The use of websites and apps for this purpose didn't exist yet!)

The summer before eighth grade, my dad told me that however much money I *earned* from babysitting and *saved* until school started in the fall, he would match for new school clothes. That fall, rather than consider the shopping to be routine, as I had in years past, I appreciated things such as the Esprit sweatshirt and Zena jeans that I was able to buy, because I knew how many diapers I had changed to help cover the cost.

Knowing what it took to get where you are, what it will take to maintain what you have, and what is needed to keep things going can instill a sense of accomplishment that can serve as a motive going forward. This is evidenced by stories of actors who wait tables in Hollywood while hoping to be "discovered" for their first big role and rock stars who tour the country for *years* while playing small clubs before landing gigs at larger venues and then stadiums once they became famous. Before online videos were an option, things had to be done in person, so patience, discipline, and determination became a way of life.

Rather than having my wings clipped, I was taught to fly. I knew that I would leave the nest two months after I turned eighteen and graduated from high school, so I became very independent, learned to be resourceful, and could improvise when needed.

If my plan A wasn't going to work, I either needed to create a plan B or figure out a way to make plan A work and adapt accordingly.

There was no rule book, per se, but the things I learned could serve as a guide in the years to come.

When I was in college, I told my grandpa that people would laugh and say I was from "the town that stinks." Yes, it was possible to smell the rotten-egg scent of sulfide from Cloquet's papermill if the wind blew the wrong way, but like so many other things in life, perspective was key. He said, "Tell people that's the 'scent of money' or 'the scent of bread and butter.'" The sulfide was used to break down wood fibers to make the paper, so the bad odor didn't bother the locals, who were grateful for the opportunity to be employed by the mill. This example of emotional grit makes me think of stories I've heard from people who lived on the "Iron Range"—a region of northeast Minnesota that has a rich history of iron ore and is located just over an hour north of Cloquet. It includes quaint towns, gorgeous scenery, and legendary underground and open-pit mines due to the area's deposits of iron ore. The stories included times when store windows, homes, and the ground would shake as blasts took place in the mines. Rather than feel frustrated, people would jokingly attribute the shaking to other things, saying, "We're feeling the economy growing" or "That's the sound of mouths being fed," as they knew where their bread was buttered too.

- ***Learning can be fun.***

When my brother and I were growing up, my grandma did things like play Monopoly with us. At the time, I had thought we were just having fun, but I later learned that she did so to help teach us how to make change. She also had us set up TV trays in the living room so we could watch *Wheel of Fortune* as we ate grilled cheese sandwiches with her and my grandpa. To me, this was fun because we could enjoy the novelty of the TV trays, but to my grandma, the time was especially well spent because watching the show could increase our vocabularies. Doing these things also had the added benefit of enhancing the bond we had with our grandparents, as the time together promoted intergenerational social connectedness. At the time of writing this book, my grandma is in her nineties, and we play a board game each week as I do her laundry. While genetically she's my grandma, in everyday life, she's also my friend.

• *Short-term setbacks can promote long-term growth.*

It is interesting how parents' clever mindsets can influence how children think for themselves.

When I was in high school, my mom worked as a nurse with residents of a memory-care unit who had dementia. In an effort to maintain some semblance of order when she got home from her demanding job, she wanted our home to be clean and tidy. However, my brother and I would still do things like leave our coats in a heap on the chair right next to the very coat closet where we should have hung them. Tired of the "visual noise," my mom told us that going forward, if our coats were laying around the house rather than hanging in the closet, she would charge fifty cents per coat. The kicker was that she wouldn't make change, so if all one of us had was a five-dollar bill, that's what had to be paid. At the time, I had thought this was ludicrous, but now, I think it's brilliant. Let's just say that we never had to pay a dime!

When I was in college, my dad would periodically take me to Target. The thought was that I could get what I *needed*. But in true Target fashion, there was also a temptation to pick out things I *wanted*. (I couldn't buy music on the internet yet, so Target was my best bet!) Rather than tell me outright what I could or couldn't buy, my dad let me do the picking, but the catch was that he wouldn't tell me until we got to the cashier stand whether or not he was paying the bill. This approach helped me learn the importance of tradeoffs and budgeting. Sometimes, I would buy paper towels and Kleenex, whereas other times, I would decide that the Kleenex could serve as both because I wanted the latest CD. Either way, I learned to think on my feet.

It's also interesting how people's professions can influence how they parent their kids. Just as my math-teacher dad had had me memorize my times tables in order to get my ears pierced, a friend of mine's dad was also a teacher who wanted to help his son think for himself. When his son, Jon, would write papers, his dad would periodically review them and say things like, "You have six spelling errors. You find them—you fix them." The key was to equip Jon to find solutions rather than providing him with all the answers.

Sometimes, wisdom isn't even having all the answers. It's knowing when to ask questions. When I was in high school, I heard that someone got in trouble for having a party once his parents came home from a weekend away camping. The problem wasn't that the house was a mess—it was that it was too clean. Within minutes of walking in the door, his parents asked, "Where are all the beer cans?" (He normally wouldn't take out the trash unless he had been told to do so.) The presence of beer cans wasn't the problem . . . it was the lack of garbage that outed him. It made me realize that in life, it's not always what you see but what you don't see that's important. After all, absence of proof isn't necessarily the proof of absence.

For example, I've met people with brain tumors or traumatic brain injuries who sometimes wish they had a cast, cane, or crutch because at least then people could see something tangible and know to cut them some slack rather than assume they're lazy or trying to be difficult. (It doesn't help that more often than not, people with brain tumors or traumatic brain injuries tend to have bandages wrapped around their head in movies or TV shows, so that's the image people expect.) Pain can be on the inside, whether it is due to someone's physical, mental, or emotional health—and they can coexist and influence each other.

• *Giving kids responsibility can promote autonomy and help them grow.*

My sense of independence was also inspired by things like going away to camp and serving as a fourth-grade school-safety patrol where I stopped traffic with my crossing-guard flag so that afternoon kindergartners could cross the street. I also started babysitting when I was eleven years old. Unfortunately, I'm not the biggest fan of thunderstorms, so I always assumed that the threatening sounds meant an ax murderer was under my bed. I needed to be strong when babysitting, though, because the loud thunder and lightning could make kids cry. Rather than get caught up in my own fear, I would become a pillar of strength for them as I said the loud sounds weren't scary because we were just hearing "angels bowling." Each time there was a menacing *boom*, the kids and I clapped and cheered because it meant an angel was knocking down the pins. The thunder wasn't the problem. It was the way we *perceived* it that could work for or against us. By being strong for them, I could make my experience positive too. Little did I know that this mindset of "flipping the script" would serve me well later in life with the health scare I never saw coming.

My dad also wanted to promote financial autonomy. My freshman year of college, he took me to his credit union so that I could open savings and checking accounts and get a credit card.

The thought was that the checkbook could make me more cognizant of how I would spend money because I would need to write it down each time I did. Regarding the credit card, he suggested that rather than using cash to pay for groceries, gas, toiletries, and other things that I *needed*, I could use the card. In doing so, my cash could earn *interest* in the bank throughout the month, and I could earn good *credit* by paying the bill. He knew that I would be tempted to also use the card for *wants*, so the credit limit was capped at five hundred dollars. I didn't fully appreciate this idea until my junior year, when I was able to use my credit score to help me buy a more reliable car without needing a co-signer. Yes, working while I went to school allowed me to make payments on the loan, but my established credit helped me qualify for it. With just one year of school left, I was beginning to fly.

> ◆ *Learning to adapt as a child can promote agility as an adult.*

The wide range of technological changes over the last fifty-plus years has been nothing short of amazing. When I was little, most people I knew had color TVs, while some still had models that broadcast shows in black and white—and people still got up to change the channel. Twenty-four-hour news channels weren't invented yet, and the ability to watch music videos 24/7 wasn't an option until the advent of MTV. I remember that once it came along, older kids at school would get up early during the week so that they could watch the videos before going to class.

I also remember thinking that my friend Colette was rich because she was the only person I knew who had a VCR. Then, I watched as mom-and-pop video stores were bought out by chains that eventually went out of business because movies could now be seen on DVDs that were mailed to people's homes. Of course, then streaming and the ability to buy or rent movies on smartphones became options.

It became a treat to watch movies over and over again because it used to be that once they left movie theatres, they were just gone. Decades earlier, the movie theatre in Cloquet had been used for vaudeville acts, such as singers, dancers, and musicians. My great-grandma Myra Cash played the piano for one of them. The performer's name was Frank Gumm. He lived about an hour away in Grand Rapids, Minnesota, where he ran a theatre that also featured vaudeville acts. One of the performers was his daughter, Frances Gumm, who would go on to change her name to Judy Garland and star as Dorothy in *The Wizard of Oz*.

There have also been material, technical advances in the world of music. From albums and eight-tracks to cassette tapes, CDs, and MP3 audio files for smartphones, the only thing constant is change. Artists' names changed too, as Jefferson Airplane became Jefferson Starship, John Cougar went back to his surname of John Mellencamp, rapper Sean Combs went from Puff Daddy to P. Diddy, and Prince changed his name to a symbol. People used to save their allowance, babysitting, or lawnmowing money to buy albums with the hope that they would like all the songs—as paying for just one song wasn't necessarily an option. (Most singles had a B-side.) To make matters even more complicated, when trying to figure out which album to buy, you had to hope that the DJ would say the name of the song or the band on the radio so that you would know which album to look for at the store. If the store was out, you had to wait even longer. There was also the gamble of hoping to hear your favorite song in a restaurant on a jukebox with a huge list of songs ahead of yours. Patience was important as instant gratification in this regard was at a minimum. Concerts were worth the wait, though, as people could express euphoria and gratitude by singing with bands in person and applauding for an encore among the flames of people's swaying cigarette lighters.

In ninth grade, I was introduced to rap or hip-hop music when a friend played his mixtape for me. It was unlike anything I had ever heard before. The genre had recently gone mainstream, but it wasn't played on my local radio yet, so the novelty of the record-scratching deejays, the reoccurring beats, and the lyrical genius of the rappers got me hooked. Initially, I thought that the clever lyrics were just cool ways to tell stories in a song—almost like fictional scripts for TV shows or movies. Without the World Wide Web, I had no clue that they could also be used to describe real-life people, places, or things outside my small, sheltered town in northern Minnesota. I was also introduced to boom boxes (i.e., portable sound systems that included features such as a cassette tape player and radio access, along with large speakers). As they played the cool songs, my friends and I would dance around the room, but the stories the songs told also introduced me to a whole new world.

When I was in college, exposure to information was incredibly limited. In the absence of access to the internet, use of social media, broadband and video chats, we used hardcopy encyclopedias that became outdated and attempted to use the Mensa-worthy Dewey Decimal System to find additional books at the library. The World Wide Web had just been invented a few years earlier, so at the time, I didn't know anyone who had access to it yet. However, I heard rumors of a few friends from high school who were able to "communicate electronically" from their colleges across the country. I would later learn that they were using what was called *email*. The ability to communicate instantly without paying the charges of a long-distance phone call blew people's minds—especially given the fact that we were raised with the idea of sending paper letters, which could take days to get to the recipients. Hotels even provided paper and pens to write them. One time, I sent a postcard from Norway to someone I was dating back in Minnesota and arrived home ten days later—before the postcard got here! It was also important to be patient when wondering how fellow classmates were years after graduation because without the advent of social media, it was common to wait *ten years* before seeing them again at the next class reunion.

In lieu of social media, we decorated lockers, passed notes, and signed yearbooks and graduation pictures. Some people wrote notes in the form of graffiti on the backs of bathroom stall doors. People also had to improvise regarding comedians because before the advent of the World Wide Web, we had to rely on the opinion of others as to whether it was worth going to one of their shows. Years later, the ability to watch videos online ahead of time allowed people to decide for themselves if they thought the person was funny before buying tickets for a show.

My freshman year of college, I used "floppy discs" and DOS to operate personal computers, and three years later, I learned how to use Windows. When I began grad school, my classmates and I used overhead transparencies for presentations, but by the time I graduated, we used PowerPoint to do the same. The technology supporting phones changed too. I used rotary, touchtone, and cordless phones before cell phones and smartphones became available when I was an adult. Before it was common to use cell phones, payphones were used when out in public, so I had to keep change on me. And if people wanted to know what the current temperature was, it was common to drive by a bank or just guess. It's also worth noting that people had to manually set their clocks for daylight savings time. (It was easy to tell when people forgot to do this in the spring because there would be empty pews at church.)

After years of witnessing all these changes in technology, I had a renewed sense of faith in medical technology's continued evolution. Rather than assume that my experience would be the same as that of someone else years earlier, I knew that in the years to come after my diagnosis, mine could be treated differently—even from hospital to hospital.

Perhaps today's questions could be remedied by tomorrow's answers.

Mentors

Just like family, mentors can provide a sense of direction—but it was up to me to take the necessary steps. While I've had different mentors over the years, the three that come to mind were all teachers of mine.

Fourth-Grade Teacher: He asked guest speakers to join our class on Fridays, one of whom was a man in a wheelchair. After sharing the story of why he was unable to walk, he asked us if we had noticed the medals pinned to his shirt. He then explained that while paraplegia was part of him, it didn't define him, so it was important to note other aspects of him beyond the chair. He then encouraged us to ask him questions about what sports he liked, which TV shows he watched, and whether or not he liked certain vegetables. It felt as though the visiting adult was conversing with us rather than giving a speech, so there was a relatable human element to the visit. Rather than view him as a *stranger* who happened to not be able to walk, he was a *person* who loved hockey but not broccoli, just like the rest of us. By providing this opportunity to learn, my teacher was able to teach us as students and give us skills for life.

High School Economics Teacher: When I was in high school, my economics teacher conducted an interesting exercise. In it, he had topics for the class to discuss as a group. The catch was that we couldn't choose which side of an argument we wanted to support—we were just given one. As a result, the exercise helped us view things more holistically and anticipate other points of view or corresponding ideas that may initially seem counterintuitive. This strategy could either strengthen your position or help you change your mind.

I thought of this exercise years later when I was diagnosed with my medical scare. Most people would naturally think that it was bad news, whereas I asked myself, "What good can come out of it?" Yes, there were times of uncertainty and doubt, but by flipping the script, I could justify my circumstance and have a sense of control. My desire to see the good in things was greater than my willingness to be blinded by fear.

Mr. D: A few months after I graduated from college, I began studying for a licensing exam in the financial services industry. The test would take hours to complete, and it consisted of a plethora of terms for securities products and services as well as the rules that govern them. Given the complex nature of the industry, Mr. D. used humor, abbreviations, and acronyms to help us learn financial terms and strategies such as butterfly spreads, tranches, and bond ladders. Don't even get me started though about arbitrage and greenshoe clauses! He also used mnemonic devices. Once, he had us draw a picture of a bicycle to illustrate the inverse relationship between the price of bonds and interest rates. If the front tire was up, that represented interest rates, while the tire that was down represented the price of the bond and vice versa. And he would help us memorize things by making us laugh. For example, when describing types of bonds, he would say "corporate bonds," "muni bonds," "government bonds," and then, in true Mr. D style, "James Bond!" The unexpected reference to the cool character from famous movies caught our attention and kept us wanting more. His style of teaching took a large volume of material with quantitative and qualitative concepts and made them easier to learn.

Over the next ten-plus years, I took more of his classes when I needed to earn additional licenses. His unique style of teaching helped me to not only pass each of them but to continue to build confidence for the next one. It also served as a great reminder that it's possible to conquer your fears rather than be intimidated by them.

Where I Was Raised

There can be a difference between *living* by people and *feeling* a sense of community with them. It is even possible to feel a sense of community with people who are separated by miles but united in spirit.

Cloquet is known as the "City of Wood" because over the years, its factories have made things such as matches and tooth-picks in addition to paper. The winters are tough, but the people are tougher because of it. The forests are thick, and hockey is king.

What we lacked in funding, we made up for in grit. There was just one high school, so the whole community would rally behind the hockey team. I remember some guys having paper routes to pay for their hockey equipment, and "ice time" was either outside on frozen ponds, at rinks in parks, or in "The Barn," our indoor ice area that wasn't heated. Our body heat, layers of clothing, the warmth of our cheers, and a few space heaters for hundreds of people had to be enough. It was a treat between periods to go into the "warming house" concession room to warm up. That area of the arena was actually heated, and we could buy warm cups of soup, hot chocolate, or coffee. The tradeoff was that it was the 1980s, so the room had a thick layer of cigarette smoke and poor ventilation. As a hockey cheerleader, I remember wearing *choppers*, leather mittens that served a dual purpose, as they kept my hands warm and also helped me clap loudly each time we scored a goal. We could see our breath in the cold air as we cheered, but no one seemed to care because we were enduring the cold together as we supported the team. I heard stories about how the locker rooms weren't heated and it was possible to see ice that formed in the cracks of the walls that surrounded the wooden stands where fans would scream each time we scored and the sound of a celebratory siren filled the cold air. Years later, I would learn that the ice had to be kept at 32 degrees and that if the arena got warmer than that, doors were opened to let in more cold air from the outside. Otherwise, humidity could freeze on the ceiling and then "rain" on the ice. I also remember hearing stories of guys older than me who couldn't afford hockey equipment, wrapping newspapers around their legs as makeshift pads when serving as goalies during games with friends. When I was little, I thought that our ice area was fancy because we went from having chain-link fencing above the boards that surrounded the ice to plexiglass. This made it easier for fans to watch the game and players to be on the ice. One time, my dad and his friend Phil saw a player get checked into the boards before flying into the air and ending up upside down with his skate caught in the chain-link fencing.

When my friend Dayna's brother was nine or ten, he and his team were playing a game at an outside rink in the nearby city of Duluth. It was so windy that day that their mom and Dayna had to stand on the back of the nets so they wouldn't slide away from the goalies. When their dad had played college hockey, his helmet had been made of leather and hadn't covered any of his face. (Not even the National Hockey League required the use of helmets until 1979, but even then, some people exercised a grandfather clause to play professionally without one.) The windchill factor could make the temperature for games feel like it was below zero, but we didn't know any different, so we just dressed for the elements and "kept our heads in the game," both on and off the ice. Guys ahead of me and behind me in school would go on to play for the NHL— guys like Corey Millen, Derek Plante, and Jamie Langenbrunner.

Great reminders that when you can't change the conditions in which you play, it's possible to figure out the *how*. In doing so, they used this hardy mindset to view problems as challenges and pursue their passion. Among other accomplishments, Millen went on to play for the LA Kings with Wayne Gretzky, and Plante and Langenbrunner won the Stanley Cup with the Dallas Stars.

Having been raised in this environment, I had my own mindset of emotional grit. An example that comes to mind was at a graduation party in the spring of my senior year of high school. One of the adults came up to me and said, "Hey, Fernjack, where are you going to school in the fall?" I mentioned that I was going to a nearby state school. He said, "Oh, you don't want to do that. The classrooms will all be huge lecture halls where it will be hard to hear."

Without missing a beat, I replied, "Well then, I'll sit towards the front."

He said, "Yeah, but your professor might have an accent, so it will be hard to understand him or her."

I replied, "Well then, I'll go to the tutoring center." After leveraging this mindset for the next four years, I thought of him when I finished my degree on time.

I also remember a time when a high school guidance counselor used a condescending tone as he told me not to go into business when choosing a college major because math "isn't your strong suit." Rather than extinguish my aspirations, the tone of his words fueled me. The tradeoff was staying up later on school nights to study for tests and sitting at my kitchen table completing homework assignments for twice as long as someone else and getting a B, but it was worth it to me. The benefit was greater than the cost, and what I lacked in math skills, I could address with discipline and drive.

Disappointment can also serve as a great motivator. I remember in high school that when people didn't make a team, get the part they wanted in a play, or do as well as they hoped in a game, they had an incentive to learn from the experience and try harder next time. These moments of self-reflection can carry over into personal and professional lives. By facing difficulties and the potential pain that comes with them, it's possible to see that *you've underestimated yourself*. Not everyone scores a goal or gets a raise or the promotion they desire. The key is to continue giving it your best and to learn as you go.

A changing of the seasons can give people an enhanced appreciation of each season—especially after a long, cold winter. The same thing can be said at the end of summer. Before you know it, daylight hours begin to shorten, leaves begin to turn vibrant shades of yellow, orange, and red, and fall is in the air. The novelty of the beautiful scenery coupled with the sounds of crackling bonfires and the taste of roasted marshmallows help to usher in the new time of year. And if you are lucky, you may even be able to look up at the night sky and marvel at the Big Dipper or the northern lights.

Even though the seasons change, Minnesotans' desire to do certain things doesn't. That's why we still hit golf balls here in the winter and go downhill skiing at a ski resort in Burnsville, Minnesota, when there's no snow. And if we feel like biking in the middle of the winter, it's possible to rent bikes with fat tires for the snowy conditions. Rather than keep us from our outside hobbies, the cold climate inspires us to think of new ways to do them.

It's easy to assume that the state with the most golf courses and players per capita should be Arizona, California, or Florida, but it is Minnesota.[1] In warmer states, people may assume that they can play all year, so there is less of an incentive to make tee times—or to keep them if it gets too hot outside. In Minnesota, people will just dress for the weather and head to the greens. I remember that one fall when a friend and I played nine holes, it was so cold outside that I wore a ski sweater over my collared shirt along with a pair of mittens—one over my golf glove—until it was my turn to swing. There was also a place in Chaska, Minnesota, where we could tee off under heat lamps and hit balls into the snow. Some people would even do it when the windchill factor was below freezing. Yes, the weather was part of the equation, but the value of the game was greater than the discomfort of the cold.

---

[1] Andrea Lahouze, "The State of Golf: A look at how Minnesota's courses are driving a new generation of golfers to the tee box," Mpls.St.Paul Magazine (May 2016), https://mspmag.com/arts-and-culture/the-state-of-golf/

Hitting golf balls into the snow in Chaska, Minnesota

When you're raised in an environment that includes the challenges of winter, it's common to develop needs, acquire certain wants, and learn what not to do in the process. For example, cans of soda shouldn't be left in a cold car because if the temperature gets too low, the contents can expand, making the can explode and leaving you with a sticky mess all over your car.

Travel can include both needs and wants, as some people fly for work whereas others fly to have a warm-weather vacation or to visit family. In 2019, I had a work trip during the "polar vortex." Arctic air coupled with strong winds brought power outages, broken water mains, and cases of frostbite. Temperatures hovered around 28 degrees below zero in the Twin Cities. As I approached Terminal One of the Minneapolis airport, I drove up to the credit card machine to pay for parking. Part of the machine was frozen, so an airport employee was standing there in the cold to help me. When I thanked him for enduring the cold on my behalf, he smiled and said, "Happy to help. I hope you have a great trip!" Wow. Rather than complain about his own circumstance, he seemed to find a sense of joy in helping me with mine. I also remember the gate agent wearing mittens to deal with the cold air coming into the airport through the jetway. During my time at the gate, I watched as she smiled and warned people that if they had children or elderly loved ones with them, they should be bundled up for the jetway because it was so cold in there that people could see their breath. Knowing that frigid air can freeze water lines, the people next to me talked about using the airport restrooms because they weren't sure if they would be able to use the ones on the plane.

Among all the uncertainty, people were still hoping we could brave the elements and fly. I'll never forget the feelings of gratitude as I boarded the flight and watched as people de-iced the plane. Passengers, including me, waved at them through the small windows as a way to say "thank you" for experiencing the cold so that we didn't have to. We weren't quite out of the woods yet, though, so when the pilot finally said we were cleared for takeoff, people began to clap their hands and cheer. The acts of many in the airline industry got us in the air that day, but their collective grit helped carry us for days to come.

Needs

While some things might seem obvious, like sleeping on a heated mattress pad or scraping ice off a windshield as the engine of a car warms up before use, there are other ways people in a cold climate get creative to meet their needs. For example, my dad and grandma have been known to put containers of food on the workbenches of their cold garages when their refrigerators or freezers were full.

Containers of food keeping cold on my dad's workbench

People like me put snow tires on their rear-wheel-drive cars and forty-pound bags of salt in the trunks for greater traction in the snow, that way they can drive the car they want all year. Things don't always go as planned though with the cold—for instance, one time, I couldn't wash dishes, take a shower, or use the bathroom at my house because the water line was frozen. At the time, my friend Donna was living with me, so we decided to shower at other people's houses and make sure that if we drank a lot of liquids on a given day, we would try to time it with using an office's or restaurant's restroom. One time, though, I had too much soda, so when I got home, we debated what to do. It was dark outside, so one option was to use the backyard, but I didn't really care for that plan, so we had to think of a plan B. Rather than feel frustrated, I got out some mixing bowls. She and I then filled them with snow, placed them in the microwave, and, after the snow had thawed, used the corresponding water to flush the toilet. Brilliant!

This same mindset of emotional grit applied when I was in college. One time, I needed to get to class, but my car doors were frozen shut, and I couldn't find my mittens. Not wanting to be late, I knew that I had to think on my feet and come up with a contingency plan. I decided to wear a pair of socks on my hands, jimmy open the hatchback, crawl over the spare tire, and drive to school. Thankfully, the cold weather didn't keep the car from starting! Wanting to exercise my bragging rights for this hilarious feat, I kept the socks on my hands and showed them to people when I got to class. As classmates began to laugh, another one chimed in and said, "That's nothing. Check out that guy over there. He couldn't find his mittens, so he *walked* to campus wearing *oven mitts*." Had I really just gotten upstaged by oven mitts? Too funny! To some, frozen car doors and walking to school in weather that warrants oven mitts would be a daunting way to start the week. To us, though, it was just Monday. When we couldn't *not* experience the cold weather, we figured out the *how*.

Wants

When people think of winter, they tend to think about things like skiing or skating, but what about making snowmen, snow angels, or snow forts? My brother and I used to also make "I love you" messages in the snow with the use of our feet. And with our uncle, we would slide off our great grandma's roof into the high snowdrifts. Some people are even more ambitious—kite skiing on icy lakes, drilling holes through ice so they can fish, or surfing Lake Superior in the middle of winter with the help of a dry suit.

Kite skiing on Minnesota's Lake Minnetonka

Temperature can be subjective. For example, some people might complain if it's 35 degrees outside, but for downhill skiers, this can be too warm because the snow may begin to get sticky and clump together on the ski slopes.

Novelty can also be subjective. When I was in college, I saw a goalie at a party with a silver tooth in the front of his mouth. I remember girls fawning over him because the silver crown meant that he had faced down adversaries and survived hockey.

The weather can inspire people to be really innovative. It can also promote creativity. In 1956, the country's first climate-controlled indoor shopping mall opened in Edina, Minnesota, a suburb of Minneapolis.

For over thirty years, the city of Wayzata, Minnesota, has hosted the Chilly Open, a golf tournament on frozen Lake Minnetonka. People use golf clubs and hockey sticks to play on the ice. Creativity is also evidenced at a personal level. For example, some people turn on the heated passenger seat of their car if they're picking up takeout food. This way, the respective entrée can be kept warm during the drive home. Over the years, I've traveled a lot for work, so I never kept a lot of food around my house. On the rare occasion that I happened to have leftovers, I would place them in the refrigerator along with my car keys. Reason being, I couldn't leave my place the next day without the keys, so by grabbing them from the refrigerator, I wouldn't forget that I had the food. Plus, I figured my keys were cold anyway when I was outside!

Some people become *snowbirds* (i.e., a northerner who moves to a warmer state in the south during the winter). For years, my grandma and grandpa would leave Minnesota to spend a few months in sunny Florida. As part of the preparation for their absence, they would open the cupboard doors that were on external walls to give pipes greater exposure to heat, put cellophane over the toilet to minimize the evaporation of water, and cancel their newspaper subscription so that strangers wouldn't see the papers piling up outside their door and know they were gone. I also heard stories of people who would purposely leave faucets dripping so that vulnerable pipes could be kept from freezing. I don't recall there being a rule book per se, just people who learned things with the gift of hindsight or from each other.

Minnesotans are really big on ice fishing. After drilling a hole through the ice of a frozen body of water, some people choose to fish out in the open, whereas others do so from an *icehouse* or *fish house* that's placed over the hole. While small in stature, the houses often have things such as heaters, bunk beds, and even flatscreen TVs. One day, I had the privilege of going with a friend and her family to their fish house. To get there, we drove out onto the ice without wearing seatbelts and with the sunroof purposefully left open. As I looked around the bay, I could see other people driving on the ice with their windows down. Initially, I was confused, but then I realized these were all precautionary measures in case we went through the ice. Augers are also used as a safety precaution; people use them to measure the thickness of the ice by drilling holes in it. Even though I could see fish houses on the lake through my living room window, this was my first time witnessing a little "village" of fish houses up close.

Fish houses on Minnesota's Lake Minnetonka

In the crisp winter air and with the ice beneath my feet, I saw people snowmobiling, walking their dogs, snowshoeing, cross-country skiing, and kite skiing—as well as kids building snow forts on the frozen lake.

While I'm tempted to write that people did these things in spite of the cold, it was actually because of it. Without the snow, we wouldn't have enough water to feed our ten thousand-plus lakes, and without the cold, there would be no ice. As I traveled for work, people from around the country would ask how Minnesotans endure winter. Yes, sometimes it can feel that way, but other times, we celebrate it. To us, it's a way of life because it's all we know. Our desire to brave the elements can be greater than our willingness to fear them. The "we're in this together" mindset that cold-weather people share reminds me of a time when I was on a ski trip. Friends and I were in a rural part of Minnesota when our SUV got stuck in the snow. One of my friends was from out of state, so she was concerned when the SUV didn't move as we took turns trying to push it out of the snow and watched as the tires would just spin in place. After about ten minutes or so, I assured everyone that someone would come by to help. Wondering where I got my confidence from, my friend asked why I was so sure that someone who didn't know us would stop to help while it was so dark and cold outside. Without hesitation, I noted that anyone driving by had probably already experienced being stuck in the snow or knew someone else who had and that they knew at any given moment, it could happen to them. Sure enough, within just a matter of minutes, a truck stopped and the two men inside helped us without even expecting so much as a *thank you*. Relatability, rather than sympathy, united us. To the naked eye, getting the SUV moving again was the sole benefit, but to the heart, *the kindness of strangers was the true gift*.

Another great example of this kind of perspective involved two ice fishermen I met by my house. As they began to test the thickness of the ice, they shared that the next step would be to walk about half a mile out on the frozen lake to set up their portable fish house, drill a hole through the ice, and start fishing. When I jokingly asked if it wouldn't be better to just stay home where it was warm, one of the guys gave me a funny look and said, "No, because then we can't smoke our cigars and razz each other about old stories from high school." To them, being out there wasn't about *having* to endure the cold. It was about *embracing* it for what it was and enjoying the brotherhood they felt while away from the responsibilities of home.

College and Grad School:

As part of my undergraduate degree, room and board were covered while school was in session, but I knew I needed to find a job if I wanted to stay with roommates between each school year. So, I began my job at Grandma's Saloon & Deli. There were tradeoffs to not living with the comforts of home, but as college kids who craved independence, college was more than academics. What we lacked in money and other resources, we made up for with improvisation and grit.

In freshman year, my roommate Denise and I experienced Minnesota's infamous "Halloween Blizzard," which brought the city of Duluth nearly forty inches of snow. Just like hundreds of schools across the state, ours was closed, and we watched as drifts of snow buried cars and caused businesses to close. There were downed power lines, and parts of Minnesota were declared federal disaster areas. I remember a carload of friends who got caught in the storm as they tried to make their way up from Minneapolis to Duluth for the holiday. What should have been a three-hour trip that morning took them well into the night. It wasn't common for people to have cellphones yet, and no one wanted to get stuck in the snow trying to find a payphone, so they relied on the radio to act as their guide. The signal wasn't strong, though, so they had no idea what they were driving into. When asked later about how they got through the dangerous drive, they said it was by singing the rock tunes of their favorite groups, such as Def Leppard, Aerosmith, and Bon Jovi.

In sophomore year, my friend Denise's mom was nice enough to knit mittens for us because we kept losing ours. As a joke, each pair was connected by a long string so that we could run it through our coat sleeves and have the mittens hang by our hands when not in use. One time, my classes ran late, so I needed to leave campus in a hurry to get to my job in Canal Park. Unfortunately, the string had not been run through my sleeves yet, so I put on the mittens with the string hanging outside my jacket. At the time, I was the esteemed owner of a little burnt-orange Dodge Colt that had a manual transmission with a loose stick shift, so whenever I changed gears, I had to keep my foot on the clutch and lean way over towards the passenger's side to move it. As one may imagine, the long string kept getting in the way as I tried to navigate the icy hills. Knowing that *not* shifting wasn't an option, I decided to wrap the string around the steering column. Little did I know that the steering column had a break in it, so the string ended up shorting out the horn. Every time I hit a bump or nearly bottomed out the car at the base of each hill, my car would beep. Some people would honk back, flip me off, or shake their fists at me. All I could do at each intersection was just raise my mitted hands to show that it was the car, not me. Rather than feel embarrassed, I owned the situation and learned the importance of rolling with things that I couldn't control. *Some of the best lessons during college had nothing to do with books.*

In junior year, I lived with three girls and two guys. One of the guys was from Greece. His parents would wire him generous amounts of spending money, so he would buy multiple versions of the same things. For example, he had two irons, so we used one to iron our clothes and the other to make grilled-cheese sandwiches. We thought we were brilliant.

After a power outage, we put duct tape on the VCR because it was blinking "12:00," and no one knew how to fix it. The tape seemed like a good contingency plan, though, especially since no one had access to internet search engines yet to research the problem. Had someone else experienced these things and just told us about them, we would have thought they were funny, but experiencing them firsthand showed us that we could remedy hassles by troubleshooting them.

Three years after I finished my bachelor's degree, I started studying for my MBA. During my last year of graduate school, I took a class in England at Lloyd's of London. I remember being surprised when I learned that some countries don't use the same name for themselves that we do. For example, the maps I saw of

Europe showed a country called "Deutschland," whereas our maps showed it as "Germany." I also learned that languages such as Farsi and Hebrew were written right to left, and I saw Japanese scripts that were written vertically.

Getting exposure to things that I didn't know existed helped me realize that there is literally and figuratively a world of possibilities—including those in the medical field. Years later, knowing this gave me a sense of hope for my medical condition.

My Professional Experience

My job hosting at Grandma's Saloon & Deli was a fun way to pay some bills, but I knew I also needed to get office experience before graduating from college. This way, I could build relationships, learn a craft, and, hopefully, line up a full-time job before finishing school. Yes, I could see job openings in the local newspaper, but contact names were important for informational interviews, internships, and potential leads for full-time positions. Not knowing anyone in the world of business, I drew upon the wisdom of one of my professors. He used to say it's important to "hunt before you're hungry," so I tried to expand my options proactively in the fall of my junior year. I scanned bulletin boards on the walls of my college campus. Then I came up with an idea while working at Grandma's Saloon & Deli. Given how much time I spent at the host stand, I couldn't help but notice how many people in suits would drop their business cards into a fish bowl near the cash register. At the end of my shifts, I would empty out the fish bowl and go through the cards for potential leads. Yes, I would then put them back!

Years later, I learned that the actor Rob Lowe had a similar approach—only instead of hoping to network with business cards, he happened to notice Liza Minnelli's luggage tag. He was ten years old, living in Dayton, Ohio, in the mid-seventies with the dream of becoming an actor. When he happened to see a luggage tag with Liza's name on it in the lobby of a hotel, he took the initiative to ask someone at the front desk where she was staying. After they gave him the room number, he went there and knocked on the door. When she answered, he introduced himself and said he wanted to be an actor. She invited him inside, and she and her then-husband listened as he explained why he wanted to be an actor. At the time, they didn't know he would become famous, but his assertive nature that day, coupled with her kindness, helped get him there.

Within a few months, I began to share a receptionist position with two other students at a brokerage firm. The office experience was more than a *job,* though, as it was a great *opportunity.* By continuing to work at Grandma's Saloon & Deli during the weekends and working the office job around my class schedule during the week, I continued to learn new things and network. For example, I learned that at the time, stocks traded in fractions (whereas now it is decimals) and that stock trades settled "T + 5" or trade date plus five business days. Years later, during the writing of this book, most stock trades settle T+2 because of advances in technology and the invention of electronic and online trading. I remember a financial advisor I worked with who printed his computer screen when it showed that the Dow Jones Industrial Average closed over 4,000—Whereas in 2020, it broke 30,000 for the first time.

As a nineteen-year-old in the world of financial services, I initially assumed that, like me, the financial advisors had all studied business in college. I later learned that wasn't necessarily the case and that each of them had their own stories of emotional grit. One person was a barber before becoming a financial advisor. Years later, I would meet someone who had sold Mary Kay Cosmetics door-to-door and at home-based parties before becoming a financial advisor. Both people had made connections in their communities, learned how to sell a product or service, experienced rejection, and found ways to move forward with the transferrable skills they acquired as part of their prior professions.

By gaining this experience and building relationships, I was able to interview for a full-time job with the firm, which I accepted just before graduation. In addition to learning more things about the industry, my new job exposed me to technology that I hadn't seen before. I also got to see firsthand how other people reacted to new tech. For example, I remember going from giving people pink slips of memo-pad paper with messages on them when they missed phone calls to transferring clients to something new called *voicemail*. I also remember hearing one of the older financial advisors panic because someone said there was a mouse in his office. He didn't know yet that the term could be used when referencing hardware for computers. Advances in phone systems and computers, in addition to acquiring the ability to enter trades electronically, helped the industry evolve into what it is today. The catch was that people, including me, needed to adapt and grow along the way.

The following year, the financial advisor I worked for had me fly to Boston so that I could participate in a due-diligence trip for annuities on his behalf. In addition to learning about the product, I learned different things about foods that I had never been privy to before. For example, during the first day's luncheon, I noticed that my soup was cold, so when the waiter was done serving the rest of the table, I asked him to come back to me so I could whisper, "Excuse me, sir, but my bowl of soup is cold. Could I please get a new one?"

He smiled and whispered back, "It's supposed to be cold . . . it's gazpacho." I had never heard of gazpacho before, so I appreciated his discretion! My roommates and I normally ate ramen noodles and frozen pizza, so the menu at the high-end hotel was way out of my league.

We didn't get access to the internet at work until later that year, so travel gave me exposure to a whole new world. I also learned a few things about food in my hotel room. When it was time for the trip to end, I stopped by the checkout counter to return my room key. Yes, there were actual keys back then. Imagine my surprise when the front desk clerk told me that I owed just over forty dollars. Not wanting to look like the travel novice that I was, I asked, "Would you mind breaking that down for me?" It was then that I learned the chocolates *on my pillow* were free, but the candy I ate from *the top of the credenza* were four to five dollars each. Who knew that the value of candy was furniture-centric? Ha! Yes, the annuity company was paying for the other expenses, but the cost of the candy was on me.

That same year, an elderly woman and her neighbor came to my office so that she could open an account. English was a second language for her, so as she handed over her paper stock certificates and bearer bonds, her neighbor helped explain that she wanted to sell them and invest the proceeds in something where she was least likely to lose money. When the financial advisor suggested that she buy US government bonds, the woman began to look really uncomfortable and assertively said, "No." Her whole demeanor had changed, and we didn't know why. It was then that she excused herself to use the ladies' room, so I asked her neighbor what had gone wrong. She explained that the woman was originally from Estonia and had lived there when it was part of the Soviet Union. She had experienced life behind the Iron Curtain until it had fallen just a few years earlier, so she was still skittish about trusting the government with her money. The neighbor also shared that the woman had intentionally kept her current stock positions in the form of physical certificates and kept tangible bearer bonds because that way, if there was a problem, she could pick up her belongings and run, just like in the "old country." Prior to meeting her, I had never heard of Estonia before because I had only learned about communism, the Iron Curtain, and the Soviet Union when I was in school. Meeting her made me realize that each of us has a story—which can influence how we perceive things. She left the office that day grateful to meet people she could trust, and I went home grateful for the people who fight to protect our freedom.

In the late 1990s, I began to work on an equity trading floor. It was during the dot-com bubble, so I saw, firsthand, history in the making. The World Wide Web was in its infancy, and people compared the surge in tech stocks to the invention and expansion of the US railroads. Because they were witnessing the massive growth and adoption of the internet, investors speculated by doing things such as buying shares on margin, seeking shares of IPOs to flip, and purchasing companies that were overvalued. Amazon had started to sell more than just books online, but the word *Google* wasn't a popular verb yet. The institutional sales guys I worked for had clients who served as portfolio managers in Europe, so they would go visit them overseas. This was when the Euro was being introduced as a new currency in Europe. When the trips were done, I had to sift through the receipts to file expense reports. The receipts would show what the cost was in the underlying currency, but there was a second column to show what the cost *would be* in Euros. I noticed that the date on the receipts listed the day before the month, whereas in the US, we do the opposite. Later, I learned that in other countries, such as Sweden, the year is put before the month and day.

It was the time of *Y2K*, the year 2000, and companies were worried that computers would process data as if it were January 1, 1900, instead of January 1, 2000. People debated if they should fly that New Year's Eve, fearing that planes would drop out of the sky. I remember that I went to a club in downtown Minneapolis so I could ring in the new year with a friend and that we enjoyed this great band that covered dance tunes from the disco era. As the crowd counted down the last ten seconds of 1999, we wondered if the lights would go out and the sound equipment would stop working as the clock struck 12:00. That didn't happen, though, so the crowd began to cheer.

Viewing the stock market can be a lesson in perspective. I remember that in 2001, the financial advisors I worked with were frustrated after 9/11 because their phones were ringing off the hook with anxious clients who were starting to panic. They had read or viewed different news stories with headlines such as, "Dow Jones Industrial Average – Biggest Point Drop Ever!" Yes, the New York Stock Exchange was a short walk from Ground Zero and, yes, the market at that time was then closed until September 17, 2001, but the biggest *point drop* at the time for the Dow Jones Industrial Average (DJIA) didn't mean the biggest *percentage* drop.

A few years later, I began to travel a lot for work. Some flights required that I get up at 3:00 a.m. or get home after midnight, but the hustle of the open road intrigued me. It was common to fly across the country and rent a car to drive through metropolitan areas such as Manhattan, Boston, Washington DC, Miami, Seattle, or Los Angeles. I also explored the Appalachian Mountains and drove across Texas, Wyoming, and Montana by myself. People are most apt to think of tourist attractions, historical sites, and landmarks when traveling. While those things all enhanced my trips, my takeaways came from the windows into everyday life that I witnessed. For example, I learned that some parts of the country use toll roads—and that I better have cash on me or think to ask for an E-Z Pass. I also saw historic cities that used roundabouts for multiple lanes of traffic, like Washington DC's DuPont Circle and came to understand that some states have roads that go by more than one name, such that the name I had been given might not be what was on the sign (e.g., by Houston, Beltway 8 is also called

Sam Houston Parkway). Given all the uncertainties of these areas that were uncharted territories for me, I learned to build in a "buffer time" by heading to the offices I was inspecting ten to twenty minutes early, just in case I had to figure out one of the noted items or face unpredictable traffic. In Los Angeles, I experienced my first time driving in six lanes of traffic. I learned to anticipate my exits way in advance so that I could be in the correct lane when I needed to exit the freeway.

Some lessons had to be learned quicker than others, though. One time when I was working in Beverly Hills, I was standing in front of my hotel bathroom mirror when one by one, the little bottles of shampoo, conditioner, and lotion began to fall off a shelf into the sink. Within seconds, I felt the ground shake under my feet. Fearing an earthquake, I Googled what to do. After standing in a doorframe for a few minutes, I wandered into the kitchen part of the suite. All the cupboard doors were open, and the dishes were close to falling on the floor. When I asked people at the office that day about what had happened, they were pretty relaxed about it because the tremor was low key and they were used to experiencing them—just like me with snow.

Where you're from can also make a difference in the laws you're used to—and can stress the need to learn about local laws and customs as you travel. One time when colleagues and I were working in Chicago, our rental car needed gas. However, when one of them pulled up to a gas pump, he didn't get out of the car to fill the tank. After a few seconds, we asked why he was just sitting there. It was then that I learned that he was from New Jersey, so he forgot for a few seconds that there are states that actually allow people to pump their own gas. Travel can definitely be an eye-opening experience—even for the most routine things.

It can also provide great reminders of the importance of not making assumptions. Had people asked me before I began traveling for work about which office visits would require the warmest clothes, I would have guessed anywhere other than those in the south. But reality began to set in once I began visiting places such as Florida, Arizona, and Texas because more often than not, office buildings, hotel lobbies, and restaurants there were over air-conditioned. It was common to see office staff with sweaters over the backs of their chairs, so I began bringing a sweater or suitcoat, too!

One trip that stands out is one I made to Montreal, Canada, which is in the French-speaking Province of Quebec. As part of my preparation for the trip, I learned how to say things such as *good morning* and *thank you* in French so that I could show respect to my hosts. Something happened that wasn't planned, though, so I had to learn from it the hard way. During my first day in the office, I was sitting in the conference room when a woman walked in and said, "It's supposed to be thirty outside today."

I looked at her and smiled as I said, "Oh, bummer—I forgot my jacket."

She replied, "You must be the American. We use Celsius here, so 30 degrees is hot." (Thirty degrees Celsius is 86 degrees Fahrenheit.) We laughed about my mistake and began to work. As I traveled there by myself, I knew that they measured things using the metric system, but I hadn't anticipated that I would see 24-hour clocks, where in lieu of *a.m.* and *p.m.*, 7:00 p.m. would read as, "19:00." I also knew there would be a different currency and that I needed to know the exchange rate, but I didn't know that in Quebec, I would see dollar amounts written with commas where we use decimal points.

It definitely helps to be a lifelong learner—traveling domestically and internationally made me realize the importance of asking questions rather than assuming I had answers.

The way I was raised, the era when it occurred, and the place where I lived, along with my educational tenure, professional exposure, and corresponding travels brought experiences that resulted in learning—and with learning came growth. Growth then provided wisdom and grit for my surprising health scare that was about to reveal itself.

CHAPTER 3

The Beauty of Gratitude

◆ ◆ ◆

"He is a wise man who does not grieve for the things which he
has not but rejoices for those which he has."
— Epictetus

I
n 2016, I had an eye appointment, as I do every year, to get
my contact prescription renewed. At the time of the exam,
my eye doctor told me that for the second year in a row, I
hadn't done as well on one of the tests. Acting on a hunch, she
said I should see a specialist. The specialist, in turn, ran more tests
and took pictures of the backs of my eyes. He said that he thought
something might be pushing on my optic nerve, so I needed to
have an MRI. I wasn't worried about it because I couldn't feel
symptoms of anything (e.g., no headaches, motor skill problems,
or cognitive inabilities). Nothing. I had the MRI the Friday of Memorial Day weekend and assumed I wouldn't get the results until
after the long holiday weekend. However, my phone rang the very
next day at 7:45 a.m., and it was a call that I never saw coming. As
I spoke with the eye specialist, he said, "Jennifer, I'm afraid I have
bad news for you. It appears as though you have a brain tumor."

It was almost as though we were talking about a third party because I was in such disbelief. I got out a pad of paper and a pen, asked lots of questions, and took copious notes. Then, literally seconds after I got off the call, I dropped to my knees and sobbed. My mind went from zero to sixty in just a few seconds as I thought, "Am I going to go blind?" and "Am I about to die?"

After about ten minutes of lying on my bedroom floor having this visceral response, I thought to myself, "I can't let this consume me . . . actually, I won't let it consume me." So I got my pad of paper and pen again and made a list of reasons why it's *positive* to have a brain tumor. It started with, "May lose weight. May meet a hot, single doctor." Then it got more somber as I wrote things such as, "Will notice the little blessings in life more frequently. Good excuse to reach out to people I haven't seen in a while." As I wrote my list, I wasn't in denial of my circumstance. Quite the contrary. I just wanted to have a voice in it, and that voice, in turn, gave me a perceived sense of control. My circumstance was overwhelming, but my desire to resist fear was greater than my willingness to submit to it.

> 5/28/16
> Positives of having a brain tumor
>
> may lose weight
> may meet a hot single doctor
> will learn to appreciate things
>   I take for granted
> will increase my vocabulary w/
>   medical terms
> will notice the little blessings in
>   life more
>   frequently
> may be forced to change my
>   hairstyle for the
>   1st time in 20 yrs
> can be a good example to others
> Good excuse to reach out to people
>   I haven't seen in awhile
> Good excuse to make every day count
> May get good parking spaces
> Good excuse to eat dessert 1st

Gratitude list after brain tumor diagnosis

I would later learn that having an "attitude of gratitude" can lower the stress hormone cortisol and influence two of the brain's "feel-good" chemicals, dopamine and serotonin. It can also reduce feelings of anxiety and depression while improving quality of sleep. I experienced these things firsthand between my diagnosis in May and my surgery in August. There were nights I would lay in bed and wonder, "Am I going to go bankrupt from medical bills? Is my life about to end as I know it?" As my eyes filled with tears, I would switch gears and think to myself, "Okay, Jenn, you can't *not* experience this, so figure out the *how*." It was then that I would count blessings until I fell asleep. By thinking, "I'm so grateful to have so much love and support" or "I'm so grateful for access to good healthcare," I could refocus as the positive thoughts helped take the edge off my experience.

One of the main reasons why I had the presence of mind to express gratitude for access to good healthcare is because in 2010, my mom had gone on a mission trip to Haiti. I was at work one day while she was away when a text came through from a number I didn't recognize. It read, "Mom is okay." Assuming I had gotten it by mistake, I almost deleted it.

A couple hours later, I received a text from my uncle, asking, "Have you heard from your mom?"

I was in back-to-back meetings, so, seeing it a few hours later, I replied, "No, she's on a mission trip."

After a few additional meetings, I read his response: "Check the news." It was then that I sat at my desk and pulled up the news online. My jaw dropped as I saw headline after headline about a catastrophic earthquake in Haiti. Thousands of homes and commercial buildings had collapsed or were severely damaged. I would later learn that the death toll was in the thousands—but on that particular day, I wondered if my mom was one of them. Remembering the mystery text I had received earlier that had read, "Mom is okay," I texted back, "Are you referring to Cathy Fernjack? If so, please tell her I love her."

A few hours later, I received a response that read, "Yes." My heart was filled with an immense sense of gratitude. I learned that the strangers who had kindly texted me were people on the same mission trip as her. Their texts needed to be short and infrequent because they were trying to conserve the battery of their phone after the corresponding power outage.

Two days later, my mom was sitting on the lawn of the US embassy when someone tapped her on the shoulder and told her to leave her belongings behind and hurry to a cargo plane that was waiting to fly them home. Though she knew the flight was going back to the US, she didn't know where the plane was going to land. After it landed at the McGuire Air Force Base in New Jersey, my mom and the other passengers waited a few hours before she and her group were placed on a bus to the Newark airport where they could catch a commercial flight home. During the bus ride, she sat by a dentist who had been volunteering with a medical group in Haiti. He told her stories of amputations that were done without anesthesia on people trapped in the post-quake debris so that they could be rescued.

After being home for four months, my mom flew back to Haiti with a group of volunteers to hold medical clinics, plant a garden at an orphanage, and help build houses for people in need. As a nurse, my mom had struggled when she left Haiti the previous time because she knew she had medical skills that people had needed, but she had needed to evacuate when she had the opportunity to do so. This was because she was sick and needed to head back to the US for medical care. By going on this second trip, she could put those skills to use. As she and the other nurse held three medical clinics, they met people who had walked for miles with their son or daughter to ask for help. My mom knew that if they had been in the US, the underlying problems could be addressed. But in Haiti after a natural disaster, they were able to just treat the symptoms.

So for me to have access to good medical care here, I'm incredibly grateful and will never take it for granted.

My tumor is called a meningioma, and it was discovered between the outer lining of the brain, the optic nerve, the pituitary gland, and the carotid artery. It was roughly the size of a golf ball and may have been growing for years, as meningiomas can grow slowly without the person even knowing they're there. There is uncertainty as to what causes them, but the numbers show that they are more prevalent in females. Less than a year before mine was discovered, I visited my aunt, who was in the hospital with a meningioma. It was surreal to think that as I sat by her bedside, we hadn't known that I had the same type of tumor in my head and that now, months later, people would be visiting me.

An attitude of gratitude during times of adversity can help people adapt, grow, and move forward. Being grateful can help people appreciate things they normally wouldn't think about. The more gratitude is expressed to others, the better they'll feel too, thereby promoting feelings of connectedness during times of need. My tumor wasn't diagnosed as cancerous, but due to its location, the surgeon removed half of it and used radiation to address the remaining part of the mass. After I rang the bell celebrating my last day of radiation treatments, my family and I handed out cupcakes with the word *Hope* on them to the radiologist and her team. As we did so, we shared that while we knew there were no guarantees in life, we were incredibly grateful to them for giving us hope. We also gave cupcakes to other patients and their caregivers. The feelings of connectedness that day are ones I'll never forget.

Cupcakes to celebrate the end of my radiation sessions

My family and I have long believed in the importance of expressing gratitude. When my grandma and grandpa turned eighty, we read tributes to them that described the things we loved and appreciated about them. We also did this for my grandma at her ninetieth birthday party. The thought was that we could share the respective accolades when they were actually in the room, rather than wait for toasts at a wedding or eulogies at a funeral. *Having the ability to see the looks on their faces was priceless.*

Gratitude is now actively encouraged in different settings. For example, some hospitals encourage their patients in intensive care units to keep gratitude journals, in which, each day, they write down something they're grateful for. That way, if there's a setback, they can read over the noted entries and find positive thoughts or enjoy positive memories. I've also heard about substance abuse programs where people are encouraged to have a "gratitude buddy." The thought is that each day they can touch base to learn from each other and feel inspired.

By having a mindset of gratitude, the brain can be trained to focus on positive thoughts and emotions, thereby reducing feelings of anxiety and apprehension. Having experienced firsthand the brain's ability to do so is yet one more reason why I believe *gratitude is a gift.*

CHAPTER 4

The Gift of Perspective and Grit

◆ ◆ ◆

"When we are no longer able to change a situation, we are challenged to change ourselves."
— Viktor Frankl

I t's one thing in life to make assumptions or have expectations, but it's another to manage them or learn from them. Perspective is key, and it can be influenced by what you consider to be "normal."

When I think of my childhood, a few things come to mind. For example, there was a time when I had been around more kittens than human babies. So, assuming they had similar experiences after they were born—and knowing that most kittens don't open their eyes until seven to ten days after birth—I asked my friend Colette's mom if her baby's "eyes were open yet." I also remember thinking that my aunt was rich because I saw multiple pairs of glasses around her house. My parents had told me that I needed to take good care of my single pair of glasses because they were expensive, so I assumed that her glasses were expensive as well. At the time, I wasn't aware yet of "readers," a.k.a. the reading glasses that can retail for less than fifteen dollars!

Perhaps my funniest assumption, though, has to do with my dad. His name is Phil, so as a child, I would wonder what was so special about his tools every time I heard other adults talk about how they "needed a Phillips screwdriver." Had adults known what I was thinking, they may have brushed off my mindset as being that of a naïve child, but at the time, these seemed like valid assumptions and questions to me because my point of view was based on the world I knew. Adults can make assumptions in everyday life too, though. I remember years ago before online dating was popular, a single friend told me that she would take notice in her grocery store of guys with handheld baskets instead of full-size shopping carts because that meant they were probably single as well. Different times!

It's easy for adults to expect other adults to have the same perspective, but if someone is new to the US, they may not know what to expect. Confusions can occur around the difference between an "emergency" room versus "urgent" care or the fact that it's common in Minnesota for anyone to use handicap-accessible bathrooms, but you risk getting a ticket for parking in a spot that is designated for people who are handicapped.

A few years ago, I met a woman who would get frustrated whenever she heard people complain about how many medications they "had" to take because at least they *could* take them. She wasn't from Minnesota, so at the time, she wasn't familiar with how to drive on icy roads. Unfortunately, she had gotten into a car accident a few months earlier, so when I met her, she was suffering from vertigo, dizziness, and nausea but couldn't take the medications she needed because she was breastfeeding.

Perspective also played a huge role throughout my brain tumor scare. A few years before my diagnosis, I heard about a Minnesota concert violinist who played the violin during his brain surgery. In doing so, the surgeons at the Mayo Clinic could know where to implant electronics to keep him from experiencing tremors as he played the respective notes. While I initially viewed this phenomenal story in a positive light, it made me nervous after I got my brain tumor diagnosis because I feared that I, too, would need to be awake during my surgery. I would later learn that the violinist, Roger Frisch, knew his degenerative disease wouldn't have just prevented him from playing the violin, the shakes would have kept him from doing his job. His desire to play had to be greater than his fear of being awake during the surgery. This incredible mindset of emotional grit justified the procedure and gave him a sense of control. I ended up not having to be awake during my surgery, so I learned a valuable lesson of not borrowing trouble or speculating that someone else's experience would be my own. Had the opposite been true, I would have drawn strength from his ability to withstand adversity with such an immense sense of courage.

My surgery lasted for nearly six hours. After that, I spent time in a recovery room and then in intensive care before moving to my own room, which I stayed in for eight days. By the time my family could finally see me, my face was swollen and bruised. My head was partially shaved, and I had nearly eight inches of stitches from the top of my head down to my left ear. I was in a drug-induced slumber, so they weren't sure what to expect from me in terms of cognitive abilities. With that in mind, my mom began to lightly rub my arm, and while doing so, she said, "Honey, it's Mom." When I smiled, they knew the wheels in my head were still turning. Rather than *fear* what might have lay ahead, my family chose to *reflect* on how far I had come. We had been told that the surgery might cause a blood clot, stroke, blindness, or even death, but none of those things happened, so my family was incredibly grateful. Due to the ominous location of the tumor, half of it was removed—with the thought that radiation could be used on the remaining part of the mass. The tumor wasn't cancerous, but radiation could kill the remaining cells.

Throughout my hospital stay, radiation sessions, and recovery period, people were kind enough to take pictures for me. That way, I had a tangible way to note my progress. In one of the pictures, it is possible to see the stitches in my partially shaved head. The next picture showed the beginnings of hair regrowth, and it is possible to see where the stitches had been removed. When I showed this particular picture to a friend of mine, he winced and said, "Jenn, no offense, but your picture is kind of creepy."

We then laughed about it, but I thought, "What a great example of perspective," because what was creepy to him was beautiful to me, as the picture showed that I was healing.

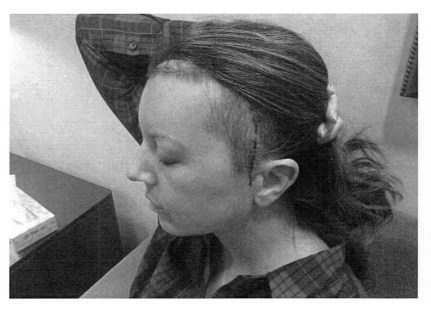

Healing from brain-tumor surgery

As part of my surgery, the trigeminal nerve was cut on the left side of my face, so I initially felt a numbing sensation across my forehead, down into my cheek, and toward my chin. Years later, my cheek still feels numb, but I choose to view it through a lens of gratitude because at least my forehead and chin don't feel that way anymore!

I knew that as part of the healing process after surgery, I couldn't lift more than ten pounds, my head had to be at an angle of at least 20 degrees when I was laying down, and I had to sneeze with my mouth open, so there wouldn't be any undue pressure on my head. Sometimes I would feel an immense sense of pressure in my head anyway if I coughed, so rather than get discouraged, I would think to myself, "At least my head doesn't hurt when I'm *not* coughing." I was also incredibly grateful that I could still do everyday things such as blink, yawn, chew, talk, and smile!

When I shared with a friend that I finished day three of my thirty radiation sessions, he responded, "Oh, no. You still have twenty-seven left to complete?"

I responded, "No, I am ten percent done!" Yes, both of us had done the math correctly, but I was viewing the pressures of the present and the uncertainties of the future as a glass that was half full. The radiation techs helped me try to stay positive. One day, I was feeling a bit down because my head was still partially shaved, I couldn't wear makeup, and I felt like a shell of my former self.

When I told one of the radiation techs that I wanted to look my best again, she said, "I think you already do."

I asked, "Why?"

She then graciously responded, "Because you're smiling."

My long, thick hair normally takes a lot of product and a long time to wash, condition, and style, so I used to complain before I was told I could lose some of it. I went into surgery knowing some would get shaved, so I didn't know how it would look when I woke up. I was also afraid that I would lose hair because of the radiation treatments. My radiation sessions were five days a week for six weeks. Each time my pillowcases were washed, I could see significantly more of my long hair in the lint trap of my dryer than usual, and I would wince each time I used a brush, wondering how much hair I would find in it. I was feeling discouraged, so once I could finally visit my hair stylist, I showed her the short hairs that were sticking up on the back of my head. I then asked if she knew when my hair would stop breaking. Imagine my surprise when she looked at them and began to smile. It was then that I learned that what I had thought was breakage was actually new hair beginning to grow, as I was healing.

It was a great reminder that things aren't always what they seem and that there's power in perspective.

Another great example of perspective took place in the world of rock music. Van Halen desired that M&Ms be in their dressing room, but "absolutely no brown ones." I remember when I was in junior high, I heard the older kids talk about how they had read in teen magazines (one precursor to the World Wide Web) that Van Halen had gone from a larger-than-life band that was cool to one that was made up of high-maintenance divas. Yes, it's true that performers are known to have special requests in their contract riders, including those for certain types of foods or drinks. It's also true that Van Halen's contract specified the preference for M&Ms, excluding the brown ones, to be in their dressing room. It's also true that if brown M&Ms were discovered there, the penalty was that the show would be canceled and the venue would still need to pay the band in full. So it's easy to see why they were rumored to be arrogant.

As with anything in life, *facts* are important, but *context* is key because not everything was as it seemed. The band wasn't a bunch of divas. They were savvy businessmen with massive stage-rigging equipment that required certain load-bearing components and specific electrical requirements. As some arenas may have a hard time meeting the demands of such equipment and as show promotors and stage managers didn't always read the contracts in full, the consequence could be delayed shows or tragic results. When the band saw M&Ms in their dressing room without brown ones, they knew that the stipulations of the contract had been read in great detail. The show could go on—with one of the best guitar players in the world and a strong sense that the equipment had been set up safely. That's not arrogance—it's brilliance.

While Van Halen's music is enjoyed by millions, their sharp business acumen was hidden in plain sight. Their story made me realize, years later, that if someone shares a negative brain-tumor story with me or if I read something negative about them online, I should pay attention to the facts but also look for context. For example, I could read that ten thousand people pass away each year from brain tumors. While that number is tragic, I would also want to know what percentage of brain tumor patients it represented. Was it 5 percent or 50 percent? I would also want to know if my particular type of tumor was included in the analysis. Again, not everything is always as it seems.

Back then, it was primarily magazines, newspapers, and television that would speculate and make assumptions. It was common for people to subscribe to magazines and just glance at tabloids in the checkout aisle at the grocery store. Nowadays, it is harder to tell the difference between the two because "news" can be commingled online. Not all websites have editors or fact-checkers, so it's important not to confuse opinions and assumptions with facts. Facts are not enough, though, as context is also needed.

Perspective can also be very subjective. When my friend Steph worked at a nursing home, she would ask residents for examples of aging, and often they would respond with things like gray hair, forgetfulness, wrinkles, hearing loss, etc. She would then respond by saying, "What about wisdom, confidence, character, and strength?"—all components of emotional grit.

The ability to persevere when facing obstacles is a mindset that is a true gift that can help anyone. It may not change your circumstance, but it can give you a sense of control or a greater acceptance of your "new normal." While most people dread having MRIs, I met a woman who had had so many of them that she pretended their loud knocking sounds were that of a symphony. She would then try to memorize them and predict the sounds that "made the songs." Doing this, she had a greater sense of control and felt less intimidated by the machine.

Some things in life can be cured or treated, but what about the things you can't get back? My grandma's neighbor enjoys public speaking but avoided it for over twenty years because of a stroke. Her essential-tremor condition also complicated things because if she got emotional or excited, her body would make adrenaline that would cause her to shake. With a desire to pursue her passion, she decided to start public speaking again. Her message of determination and hope also gave others a voice. A friend of mine used to love playing the piano and guitar but couldn't do so once he began to lose the dexterity of his hands due to a surprising diagnosis of ALS. Rather than not be able to play music, he decided to switch instruments and began playing the harmonica. He even played "Happy Birthday" to one of the nurses who was helping him with his ALS. Yes, the disease was changing his body, but he wasn't going to let it affect his spirit.

Another great example of emotional grit comes from a financial advisor I met who lost his sight when he was in college decades earlier. As he was studying for exams, he and his roommate heard two gunshots fired outside their home. One of the shots came through the wall of the house and blinded him instantly. Not one to be defeated, he began learning braille three days after the tragic event, and within three months, he was back at school with the help of recorded books. He then went on to earn a master's degree and licenses for the financial-services industry.

My brain tumor had been pushing on my left eye, so for years, my left eye has protruded a bit from that side of my head. Before my surgery, I hadn't thought twice about how it looked because most people's faces aren't symmetrical. Wondering if the soft tissue that was cut during my surgery would make my eye stick out even more, I knew that I could feel self-conscious about it or try to remedy it the best I could. So I walked over to a department store in downtown Minneapolis, bought some new makeup, and asked the makeup artist to show me how I could use it to make my eyes look more even. Most people probably wouldn't even notice the placement of my eye, but taking the initiative to learn how to apply my makeup helped me regain my confidence in how I presented myself to others. *Knowledge can provide a perceived sense of control when facing the unknown.* Other examples include planning for a wedding, studying for an exam, or preparing for a job interview.

Two months after my radiation sessions ended, I was on an airplane for a work trip. Even though I had been told it was safe for me to fly, I wondered if the change in cabin pressure would hurt my head. As the plane began to pull away from the jet bridge and taxi to the runway, I could feel it begin to accelerate and hear the rush of the engines as they began to roar. Fearing the pain that might be before me, my eyes began to fill with tears. Knowing that I couldn't *not* experience takeoff, I had to figure out the *how,* so I sought a diversion to clear my mind. Thankfully, the woman next to me was wearing cute shoes, so I asked her about them, and we began to laugh about how even though they gave her blisters as she ran around airports, she could justify them because they were cute. The kindness of the stranger, the novelty of the shoes, and the laughter from her relatable story made me feel good and helped me forget what was going on around me. The plane was already in the air, and I had never even felt the wheels leave the ground. When I had boarded the flight that day, I had viewed my head as a potential liability when it was actually an asset, as the "feel-good" chemicals of my brain saved the day.

One of my favorite stories of someone being able to think on her feet is that of my mom. Since 1986, she has gone on mission trips all over the world, including visits to Kenya, Haiti, the Dominican Republic, Guatemala, Nicaragua, Canada, and Mexico. Of the fifty-plus trips, at least thirty of them have been to an orphanage in Reynosa, Mexico. There, she watched the children grow and did things such as baking cookies with them, providing lots of hugs, and tucking them in at night after she read their favorite stories. For one trip in particular, she wrote a letter to someone at General Mills, who she had never met, to see if they would donate packages of cookie dough. Imagine her surprise when she he received an entire case. Knowing that the needs and wants of the caregivers were also important, she encouraged them to share their struggles and actively listened as she validated their feelings. During one of the trips, she had noticed that some of the adults and children needed new shoes. She wanted to help, but given the fact that a lot of their shoes were either worn through or donated, it was hard to know what the correct sizes were to buy. Not one to be deterred, she had to think of a plan B, so she found pieces of paper and began to trace their feet. Noting what she was doing, others jumped in and began to trace feet too. She then brought the drawings across the border to a Walmart and bought the shoes. Her non-profit, Mother's Touch Ministry, is only a party of one, but her efforts and those of her donors continue to touch and inspire people to this day . . . including me.

CHAPTER 5

Creativity in a Pandemic

◆ ◆ ◆

"We will either find a way or make one."
— Hannibal

Springtime is normally somewhat predictable in that snow melts, the end of the school year is near, and the days begin to get longer; however, the spring of 2020 brought with it a global pandemic that people didn't see coming. I remember that firms in downtown Minneapolis stopped having most of their employees go to the office, and it became common for people to start working from home with the help of virtual meetings. States began to mandate that people "shelter at home." In addition to fearing the pandemic, people were also afraid of the unknown. To make matters worse, there was a shortage of supplies like masks, hand sanitizer, and other household goods, so speculation led to hoarding. Not knowing what caused COVID-19 or how it could be spread, people were encouraged to wash their hands frequently and only leave their homes if necessary. Masks and social distancing then became the norm, but fear of the unknown, coupled with the longing for a vaccine, made people crave a sense of normalcy and control. Knowing that people were feeling frustrated, anxious, and alone, radio stations across the country, including some in

Minnesota, began to play the national anthem at 12:00 p.m. on March 23, 2020. It was a sign of solidarity and a moment that united people during a time of need.

Minneapolis park water fountain, March 23, 2020

Streets of downtown Minneapolis, May 2020

Parents took on the challenge of helping their children with distance learning, and in ads for nannies, families would ask applicants if they had already had COVID-19, hoping that lightning wouldn't strike twice. People who didn't have wifi in their homes had a hard time getting the access they needed because the libraries, restaurants, schools, and malls they relied on were closed initially, with restaurants only allowing orders for takeout and delivery. In addition, fresh vegetables were being plowed back into the soil because the hotels, restaurants, and schools that normally needed them were closed.

Even the most routine things became luxuries. Hair salons weren't considered an "essential" business, so initially, they were closed. People who would normally look very professional at work joked on virtual calls about hair being longer than usual and grays showing that were normally covered. I know that I went for five months without visiting my salon. I only put gas in my car once between March and May of that year since I couldn't really go anywhere other than the grocery store or other businesses whose goods or services I truly needed. I remember that once my eye doctors' office could conduct routine checkups again, I called them from the parking lot to let them know I was there. They could then ask me COVID-related questions or at least let me know when I could enter their practice. The staff wore masks, and so did I.

Precautionary measures were also taken by my veterinary clinic. I had to call them from the parking lot to let them know that they could come outside to get my cat, and I paid for the visit by credit card over the phone. Knowing that they were at risk of exposing themselves to COVID-19 so that pets could get the help they needed, I wanted to say "thank you" but wasn't sure how. So I made a sign and held it outside the window of the clinic. Their touching reactions made me feel good during this dark time.

Places of worship dealt with closures and restrictions. A colleague of mine told me that her church, not wanting the airborne virus to spread, wasn't allowing the congregation to sing after they were allowed to meet again in their sanctuary. My church offered virtual and outside services before gathering indoors again. Once we were there in person, people had to wear masks, and we were spaced on the pews with respect to the need for social distancing. People could text their offering payments to the church or submit them to kiosks outside the sanctuary, but offering plates weren't passed between congregants, and there was no shaking of hands— just waving at each other during that time of the service. People didn't seem to mind the restrictions because we were just grateful for the sense of community during a time when it was easy to feel empty and alone. People were also advised not to cheer at Super Bowl parties or yell and scream on theme park rides because of the risk of spreading the airborne virus.

Similar restrictions took place in Europe. For example, the Scottish government updated its guidelines for restaurants, bars, and cafes, "encouraging" the respective establishments to "challenge" anyone who began to sing and to stop playing music and mute their televisions so that people weren't tempted to yell at them during sporting events. From churches in the US to bars in Europe, when people wanted to congregate again, the risk of COVID-19 couldn't be eliminated, but it could at least be reduced—even if that meant not cheering, yelling, screaming, shouting, or singing.

In December of 2020, I was thinking about downtown Minneapolis and missing the friends, colleagues, former colleagues, and local merchants who had provided a sense of community for me over the last twenty years. Wondering what I was missing, I asked someone who was still working downtown to take some pictures and a video for me. I had heard that downtown Minneapolis had become a ghost town, but the pictures and video he sent me actually made things real. One place that was particularly sad was the Crystal Courtyard of the IDS Center. There was a Christmas tree, but the courtyard was eerily quiet. For years, while enjoying the sounds of holiday cheer, I had witnessed the hustle of people holiday shopping there or meeting others for lunch. Christmas carols would be sung by choirs in the courtyard or played by orchestras, and it was common to hear bell ringers raising money for the

Salvation Army. On this day, though, during the pandemic, there was just silence and a room that was nearly empty. When I first saw the video, I was taken aback by feelings of loss for the world that had been taken from me so abruptly just months earlier.

IDS Crystal Courtyard, December 2020

There were stories of people unable to have funerals with family and friends and of schools without basketball tournaments, proms, or commencement services because people couldn't risk spreading or getting the virus. Without hospitals allowing visitors, patients would receive much-needed chemotherapy treatments and MRIs as their worried loved ones sat in cars in the parking lot. Some patients were even given higher dosages of radiation over fewer treatments because they risked getting COVID-19 at the hospital. At the time, there was uncertainty as to how people could catch the virus and in what ways it could be prevented and remedied, so it was best to weigh options and proceed with caution while people hoped for a vaccine.

While it was easy to get caught up in the cancellations, closures, and restrictions of the pandemic, it was interesting to note some positive things that happened. For example, some businesses were actually doing better *because* of the pandemic. For example, a UPS store in downtown Minneapolis that serviced returns for people and small businesses who shopped online saw an increase in demand when online purchases began to happen more frequently. The store also experienced an increase in demand when financial services firms began to have their employees work from home. The continued need for fingerprinting and the notarization of documents was now being done by the store on the firms' behalf.

Businesses learned to adapt and improvise as state-by-state restrictions for COVID-19 ebbed and flowed. By June 1, 2020, Minnesota restaurants were able to serve people on their patios, as opposed to just offering delivery or pickup. I remember the date because it is my birthday—my friend Justin and I went out to celebrate not only the occasion but also the fact that we could leave our homes to eat some of our favorite foods. For the first time in my life, I heard a host ask if we wanted to use paper or virtual menus as she sat us at a socially distanced table. (When I had hosted in a restaurant years ago during college, I just asked people if they wanted "smoking or non" as I sat them.) The paper menus were recycled, and the virtual menus could be accessed with the use of our smartphones, by going to the restaurant's website. The servers wore masks and gloves, and the straws were wrapped in paper. The restaurant couldn't eliminate the risk of COVID, but they could reduce it by thinking outside the box and adapting to the new normal.

By January 2021, Minnesota restaurant dining rooms were closed again, so rather than just offer delivery or takeout, a bowling alley in Maple Lake, Minnesota, decided to improvise using fish houses. By setting them up in their parking lot, the restaurant could allow customers to enjoy the camaraderie of eating in them as the server took orders and delivered food and drinks through the small windows. The fish houses contained space heaters, so it felt almost like camping. As my friend Andrea and I enjoyed the novelty of our fish house, we learned about the "BYOF program" that encouraged people to "Bring Your Own Fish House." As we were leaving that day, we could see someone with a flatbed truck doing just that. My drive to the bowling alley had taken a little over an hour, but the server told me that other people had driven there for *hours*, including a couple who liked to fish that had driven all the way from North Dakota. Yes, there was a pandemic and it was cold outside, but the novelty of the idea provided a sense of community and attracted people from all walks of life. The same thing could be said of a ski resort in northern Minnesota where skiers could order their food in the ski lodge but had to eat it outside. People were wearing warm ski clothes, so I could see them eating outside, but others had actually brought fish houses for their makeshift dining rooms. The cluster of fish houses at the base of the ski hill served as a reminder that even though we were experiencing a pandemic, people could still try to have fun in spite of it.

Fish houses at the base of a ski hill in northern Minnesota

Restaurants in the suburbs of Minneapolis took a similar approach. When they couldn't house customers indoors, they covered outside tables with plastic "bubbles" that looked like igloos and placed space heaters in them.

Covered tables outside a restaurant

Baby showers and funerals became improvised too. I know that my mom participated in a virtual baby shower where people ordered their gifts online ahead of time with the thought that they could be sent directly to the host. Guests could then celebrate by watching the mom-to-be open her gifts virtually from the safety of their homes.

On a more somber note, I also heard of a celebration-of-life service for someone during the pandemic. The family was allowed to be at the funeral home in person for the eulogies and singing, but the other seats in the room were empty. They could see other people, though, with the help of virtual reality and a screen. When the service was done, people could drive through the parking lot to wave or hold up a sign to show respect and support for the family.

Amazing stories of emotional grit came from hospitals around the world. Lonely patients with COVID-19 were struggling to live in the isolation of intensive care units, so two nurses in Brazil wanted to help. As part of their plan, the nurses filled latex gloves with warm water, so they could use them to simulate human touch. After tying them off like water balloons, the nurses placed the inflated gloves on each side of a patient's hand with the fingers linked between those of the patient. The unconscious patients could then feel a sense of comfort, as if someone was holding hands with them. Experiments have shown that simply holding someone's hand lessens the emotional response in the brain to perceived threats. In addition to promoting the mental and emotional well-being of the patients, the technique also helped to increase blood flow.

One of the most selfless stories I heard during the pandemic involved a state trooper from Minnesota. When a cardiologist from Boston, Massachusetts, was on temporary assignment in Duluth, Minnesota, she got pulled over for speeding by Minnesota State Trooper Brian Schwartz. Noticing on her driver's license that she was visiting from out of state, he asked her what she was doing so far from home. He also noticed what appeared to be two used N95 masks next to her. She had been working in a quarantine unit for Essentia Health that included COVID-19 patients, so the masks were paramount. They were also in short supply. As she tried to apologize and thank him for letting her off with a warning, she reached for her driver's license. It was then that she realized he had given her five N95 masks that were meant for him. This act of kindness during such a foreboding time—when the avenues of viral transmission were not known and people were dying—united two people and inspired the world as the story went viral.

People began to share positive things they had experienced firsthand, heard from a friend, or read online. Examples of these stories include a little girl and her dad who put on costumes to take out the garbage and residents in Dallas who sang together from apartment windows. People were grateful for the ability to have virtual doctor appointments. And nursing homes started offering virtual calls for lonely residents so that they could not only speak with their families but actually see them. I learned about schools in Waseca, Minnesota, that were using school buses as mobile learning stations for students without access to the internet and a Twin Cities restaurant called Italian Eatery that sold t-shirts to support their staff. The t-shirts read, "Pasta Unites," and if someone bought one, it could be worn to one of their locations to get a free dish of pasta—once the restaurants could open again.

My own unique circumstance involved public speaking. Within months of my brain-tumor surgery, I began giving speeches about emotional grit in conference rooms, auditoriums, and other venues. Once the pandemic hit, I switched gears by giving them virtually. Needless to say, it was a bit surreal to start giving speeches in front of my computer while sitting at my dining room table. One time, I was being filmed, so the audience was told they could listen through their computers without showing themselves. I then gave my speech to an audience I couldn't see. Definitely one for the books!

With the uncertainties of COVID-19, people began hoarding groceries to the point where some items were hard to find and stores had to limit the number that people could buy at once. Toilet paper was especially scarce, so one of the cashiers at my local grocery store told me that she was going to ask her neighbors if she could have some of theirs. They were snowbirds who were in Florida for the winter, so she figured that they would have paper products they weren't using in their Minnesota home. A few weeks later, the grocery store was completely out of toilet paper, so as the same cashier rang up the litter I was buying, I said, "It's so sad that you're out of toilet paper because people are hoarding it."

She replied, "At least your cat can go to the bathroom."

I smirked. "What makes you think I have a cat?" We then laughed as I paid the bill. The fear of the unknown had prompted the hoarding, but the pandemic wasn't going to rob us of joy.

Holidays were improvised too. For months, my grandma's senior living building didn't allow guests, so families began to communicate differently. One of the building's residents turned one hundred during the pandemic, so their family celebrated by writing "Happy 100" in the snow outside her window. On Christmas Eve, I held a large "Merry Christmas" sign outside my grandma's fifth-story window when it was below zero outside. The gesture took just a matter of minutes, but the fond memories will last a lifetime.

The Minnesota State Fair normally draws a crowd of hundreds of thousands of people, shoulder to shoulder each day as they enjoy the farm animals, deep-fried foods, concerts, fireworks, and rides. Instead, in 2020, there was a State Fair Food Parade at which food vendors could serve people who were social distancing in their cars. Tickets for the historic event sold out in a matter of hours. Yes, people enjoyed the food, but they also craved a sense of normalcy. The fairgrounds offered a taste of freedom as people were grateful to be out of their homes doing something they loved and exercising emotional grit.

Chapter 6

Finding Strength in Disabilities

◆　◆　◆

"The only thing worse than being blind is having sight
but no vision."
— Helen Keller

Some of the strongest people I've heard of or met have a disability. When I was growing up, my mom wanted my brother and me to build an awareness of people with disabilities so that we could appreciate and respect the challenges they faced, while noting that they had feelings just like us. I remember learning that I should sit down when speaking with a friend of my mom's who had multiple sclerosis so that she wouldn't need to look up at me from her wheelchair. I also learned that people don't have to feel hindered by their disabilities because these can help drive them.

Years later, I would meet a financial advisor who injured his spinal cord in a terrifying mountain-biking accident. Longing for his old way of life, he was incredibly grateful when he could go back to work. By being able to service his clients, he regained his sense of purpose. This was made possible by his wheelchair-friendly desk and an aid who helped him get to and from work and assisted with different tasks throughout the day. When I spoke with him in his office, I felt an immense sense of gratitude because it was such an honor to meet him. All morning, his colleagues had spoken so highly of him and his emotional grit, and the feeling of inspiration was very contagious.

I also felt inspired when I saw people "adaptive skiing" at a ski resort in Minnesota. With the use of specialized equipment, people with physical disabilities can strengthen their motivation, confidence, and balance by sitting in a bucket-style seat with skis underneath it. An adaptive skier can turn by using handheld outriggers or moving his or her head and shoulders.

I'll never forget one day when I was eating lunch with a friend in downtown Minneapolis. My phone began to buzz. It was people texting me about the passing of Prince. I was in complete shock. We were just blocks away from First Avenue, the nightclub made famous by him in the movie *Purple Rain*. Paisley Park, Prince's home and recording complex, was just fifteen minutes from my home. Years ago, I had seen him perform there. Prince didn't come on stage until after midnight, but the show was worth the wait. The set list included music from the *Purple Rain* soundtrack, so the upbeat tempos, guitar solos, and crazy lyrics brought back fond memories of junior high, high school, and college. He was just twenty-five when *Purple Rain* was introduced to the world and made history. Similarly, The Beatles were all in their early twenties when they had their first No. 1 US hit. Michael Jackson was twenty-four when the album *Thriller* was released, and its worldwide sales went on to make it the best-selling album of all time. All great reminders that age doesn't need to inhibit ambition.

In an interview with Tavis Smiley, Prince shared that he was teased as a child for having epileptic seizures and that early in his career, he tried to compensate for that by being as "flashy and noisy" as he could.[2] Years later, in 2018, he was honored by a concert in the lead-up to the Minneapolis-hosted Super Bowl. It was 9 degrees when I joined thousands of people on the frozen streets of downtown to hear Sheila E., Morris Day, and The Revolution perform the outdoor tribute concert. It was possible to see the breath of strangers in the cold air as we sang along to the great tunes and danced in our boots. There were rumors that problems with some of the equipment on stage were due to the frigid air. The guys next to me had flown in from Florida. They had never experienced cold temperatures like that before, so they had bought warm clothes for the show. Imagine my surprise when they told me that they thought the cold was "cool" because it was part of the "experience" as they honored the memory of Prince, the artist who was once teased for being different and was now celebrated because of it.

Actor Henry Winkler played the rebellious, leather-jacket-wearing character called The Fonz on the TV show *Happy Days*. It ran on ABC from 1974 to 1984 and made him a star. Henry knew the character, with his smooth pompadour haircut and swagger, would typify the essence of confidence and cool. Of course, the motorcycle and the bad-boy persona attracted the ladies too. What Henry didn't know though, was that he had dyslexia, because the diagnosis didn't come until he was thirty-one. After years of receiving blows to his self-esteem from people who called him names and questioned his ability to apply himself, he felt that his efforts were finally validated. He struggled when trying to read the scripts, but he could still pursue his passion of acting. The emotional grit in doing so helped him navigate the stage. Yes, The Fonz wore the leather jacket, but the coolest guy in the room was Henry Winkler.

---

[2] (Biography.com Editors, "Prince Biography," Biography.com (October 2019), https://www.biography.com/musician/prince

Other people in the entertainment industry have faced similar challenges. Tom Cruise and Steven Spielberg both have dyslexia yet have gone on to become a successful actor and director, respectively. When asked about his dyslexia on the TV show *The Big Interview with Dan Rather*, singer John Mellencamp said he's okay with it because it makes him a "better listener." The talented British singer Adele gets stage fright yet continues to push through it by touring throughout the world, and James Earl Jones got through years of stuttering to become the famed voice of Darth Vader.

Familial and community support are extremely important. In 2020, I participated in a fundraising walk for Brains Together for a Cure, an organization in Rochester, Minnesota, that helps fund innovative research for fighting brain tumors. As part of the event, people were encouraged to wear customized t-shirts to publicly acknowledge their support of brain tumor patients and survivors. The shirts were also worn by some in honor of a friend or family member who had passed away in their brain tumor journey. It was great to see the different designs. My favorites were simple, yet they said a lot. As people walked ahead of me, I could see t-shirt after t-shirt that read on the back, "I'm with Jim." Then I saw one that read, "I'm Jim." The shirts were meant to support him, but the unity of their captions also inspired others.

It is interesting to see how in learning about others, whether those experiencing paralysis, seizures, dyslexia, stage fright, a speech impediment, or a brain tumor, we can learn about ourselves, as the strength of resolve can be greater than the weight of worry.

Chapter 7

The Rewards of Kindness

◆ ◆ ◆

"I've learned that people will forget what you said, people will
forget what you did, but people will never forget how
you made them feel."
— Maya Angelou

From sharing toys to carrying someone else's books or giving a stranger one's seat on a bus, there are ways that children can be encouraged to do nice things for others. Parents can get creative in this regard. A former colleague of mine would have her daughter choose which book they should donate to their local library when she got a new one. My friend Colette would bundle up her three boys for the cold so that they could ring bells for the Salvation Army while Christmas shoppers were nearby and snow was in the air. By instilling these values in kids when they are younger, kids can learn from them as they get older. Most people assume only the recipient of an act of kindness benefits, but the person who initiates it can benefit too, as can anyone who sees the act firsthand or learns of it later. The acts can actually trigger the brain's "feel-good" chemicals such as oxytocin, dopamine, and serotonin. Oxytocin can help build social bonds and trust while lowering blood pressure. Studies have also shown that dopamine can give people what's called a *helper's high* when doing something nice and that serotonin can help regulate mood. In addition, helping others is believed to increase levels of substance P, which is an endorphin-like chemical that can help reduce the perception of pain.

Experiencing or learning about acts of kindness can give people a renewed faith in humanity and inspire them to help others. I've heard stories of people going through toll booths and paying for the cars behind them, of layaway accounts for people's Christmas gifts being paid for anonymously, and of the domino effect of one car after another paying for the car behind them in fast-food drive-throughs. In December of 2020, a customer of a Dairy Queen in Brainerd, Minnesota, decided to anonymously pay for the vehicle behind him, which inspired *over nine hundred others* to do the same.

The COVID-19 pandemic was making people feel isolated and anxious, so the opportunity to unite with strangers this way brought some people to tears. With the help of social media, customers found out that enough funds had been donated to keep the chain going into the next day, so more cars followed suit. The three-day venture paid for roughly ten thousand dollars in sales and inspired others as their acts of kindness made headlines around the country.

Acts of kindness that I've experienced, witnessed firsthand, or learned about through my travels continue to have a positive effect on me to this day.

When I was in eighth grade, my friend Denise and I were hanging out upstairs at my house when we heard my mom talking to someone downstairs. Wondering if someone had stopped by to visit, we crept down the stairs and peered over the railing. We could see my mom standing in front of the phone book as it lay open on our kitchen table. As she did so, she was speaking over the phone to someone at a radio station. We overheard her reference to the station's talk show, on which they were asking people to share what they were doing for Christmas. One of the listeners who called in said that she had no place to go because she was divorced without kids, her parents had passed away, and she was estranged from her brother, who lived "somewhere in Wisconsin." It was then that my mom called the station and said, "I know you can't give me the caller's contact information, but please give her mine. She can come to my house for Christmas." Denise and I didn't say anything, but our expressions spoke volumes. The caller never joined us because another listener knew her brother and connected them for the holiday meal. While the gesture was intended for a stranger, the benefits could also be felt at home.

Years later, my classmates and I got together for a reunion just before my brain-tumor surgery. I didn't tell very many people about it, though, because I didn't want to risk bringing down the mood of the event. My classmates knew that I was okay with them sharing the news, so word must have gotten around the room because a few months later, I received a check in the mail. Someone must have started asking people if they wanted to make a contribution toward my medical expenses. To this day, I don't know who the contributors were because they did so anonymously.

The generosity and kindness of their selfless acts are things I'll never forget.

Acts of kindness I have witnessed, experienced, and heard about in my travels have made a huge impact on me. For example, I learned about a couple in California who stood side by side as they served customers from their charming donut shop. That changed when the man's wife was admitted to a rehab facility for an aneurysm. Her husband wanted to show support by spending time with her at the facility, but he still needed to run the business and pay the bills. News of their circumstance spread throughout the community, and customers wanted to help. One by one, they would come into the shop and buy a dozen donuts, even if they wanted just one. The thought was that if the inventory was gone early in the day, the husband could spend more time with his wife as she tried to heal—a great example of how a community can come together to show kindness . . . one donut at a time.

In 2019, Wayne Wilson passed away. As a veteran of the Vietnam war, he was to have a service with full military honors and a military salute. He didn't have any surviving family members, though, so the thought was that the service would be small. However, when intern Drew Mickel of Brown Funeral Home and Cremation Service in Niles, Michigan, heard the news, he decided to invite the public so they could help honor him. More than three thousand people showed up from across the country, including people from as far as Iowa, Tennessee, and Florida. While they weren't technically relatives, their feelings of respect for Wayne made them family.

At the Wilkes-Barre/Scranton International Airport, I saw a "wishing tree" where passengers could stop to make a wish for themselves, family, or friends. As I looked at the tree, I could see little pieces of paper that were tied to it with wishes written on them. Assuming that people would wish things for *themselves*, I was blown away as I read things such as, "All our troops come home safely," and "Good health for everyone." In a public place where people were self-contained and on the go, it was beautiful to see that people were wishing the best for each other.

Wishing Tree at the Wilkes-Barre/Scranton International Airport

In Dallas, Texas, there was a middle school that wanted to host "Breakfast with Dads," but they weren't sure if enough dads or volunteer mentors would be there. Hoping to draw attention to the cause, a request for volunteers was promoted through social media. It asked for about fifty men to come serve as mentors for the boys. Imagine their surprise when the day of the breakfast, nearly *six hundred* men showed up to show support for the students and serve as mentors. This act of kindness benefited the students that day, but the underlying virtues will serve them well as they experience the world around them.

Acts of kindness and altruism can touch people on a global level, and the appreciation for the values that underlie them is timeless.

During World War II, Sir Nicholas Winton organized the rescue of over six hundred children (mostly Jewish Czechoslovakians) who were heading for Nazi death camps. The operation was called "Czech Kindertransport," and it provided them with safe passage to Britain. For decades, Winton didn't tell anyone what he had done, not even his wife. However, in 1988, she found a scrapbook in their attic dating back to 1939 that contained a list of the children's names, pictures of them, and even letters from some of their parents. Later that year, the BBC program *That's Life* wanted to host a reunion show for Winton. In it, he was surprised to learn that one of the children he had rescued, now an adult, was sitting right next to him. As he wiped tears from his eyes, the show's host asked if there was anyone else in the audience who he had helped save. It was then that people who were sitting all around him began to rise as an expression of gratitude. Winton's desire to save the children was greater than his willingness to protect himself, and his selfless mindset has now inspired emotional grit around the world.

When the United States closed its airspace after the terrorist attacks of 9/11, a small airport in Gander, Newfoundland, opened its runways for the thirty-eight planes and seven thousand stranded travelers who were on transatlantic flights that were forced to land immediately. The small community of fewer than ten thousand people wanted to help by opening their homes, cooking wonderful meals, and letting people use their cars. The town didn't have hotels or restaurants to accommodate the people, so rather than viewing them as strangers, the visitors were treated as guests in individual dwellings. The people of Gander and neighboring fishing villages also provided cots for people to use in places such as schools and churches. On a date that can be remembered each year with immense negativity, it's comforting to know that acts of kindness helped people in need as doors and hearts were opened for strangers who became family.

It's common nowadays to get text messages as reminders for medical appointments or perhaps to pick up a prescription, but in Sweden, people who donate blood get a "thank you" text when their blood is given to a patient. This personifies the need and helps the donor feel good, giving them a helper's high for what they did and thereby giving them an incentive to do it again.

Researchers theorize that altruism lessens negative experiences by providing a sense of control and meaning. For example, experiments have shown that people giving blood say the needle hurts less when giving blood to earthquake victims. The same could be said for me when I was getting an IV of dye in my arm for some of my MRIs. By pretending I was doing so on behalf of my nephew, who was four at the time, I felt good for "protecting" him. This mindset helped me stay strong and kept from fainting.

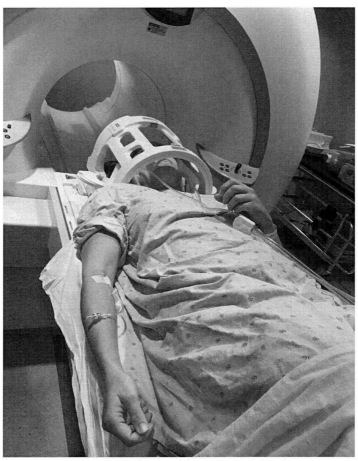
Entering an MRI machine with an IV of dye in my arm

One time, someone on one of my work trips got stuck in a hotel elevator for a prolonged period of time. She was claustrophobic, so normally, a situation like this would have made her panic. She stayed strong, though, because she helped a stranger who was also claustrophobic. By playing music on her smartphone, she created the opportunity for them to listen to great songs, share memories associated with them, and quiz themselves on lyrics as a means of distraction. In helping the stranger, she also helped herself.

When thinking about ways that initiating acts of kindness can give you a helper's high, it's important to consider the fact that others can also benefit from this high. I'm two years older than my brother, and I remember that when I would visit him and my mom during holiday breaks from college, she would say that it "felt good to have her baby chicks under one roof." Over the years, my grandma has said the same thing about having her children and their families together at the same time for holiday meals. When my mom or grandma made our favorite meals or baked one of their delicious treats, the acts didn't just benefit the recipients, as they also made them feel good for doing so.

My friend Jen also witnessed the importance of letting someone do something nice. Her sister was a nurse at a rehab center, so when we were in junior high, she had Jen visit the center with her when she had a staff meeting. The thought was that Jen could meet Jack, a resident with quadriplegia. He had been in a car accident in his mid-twenties that had ended in paralysis. Because of his injuries, Jack was unable to talk, so Jen learned how to read his lips and interpret the clicking sounds he made for *yes* and *no*. *Yes* was one click and *no* was two. Jack was incredibly grateful for everything people did for him, so Jen began visiting him about once a week when her sister needed to be onsite. The frequency of her visits allowed her to watch as the medical personnel joked around with him, swapped stories, and treated him like a *person* rather than just a name on a chart. As a reflection of his appreciation, Jack would buy pizza for the staff and have it served at pizza parties during their breaks. By accepting his invitation, the staff gave him a helper's high and made him feel like one of their own.

Acts of kindness don't need to be expensive. They can be low-cost or free. Doing things such as holding a door open for a stranger, smiling at someone, expressing gratitude, or paying someone a compliment can go a long way. Plus, it's comforting to know that during times of adversity, kindness can foster emotional grit.

CHAPTER 8

The Wonder of Music and Arts in Healthcare

◆ ◆ ◆

"Where words fail, music speaks."
— Hans Christian Andersen

Music provides a medicinal value that can benefit people physically, cognitively, and emotionally. I experienced this firsthand through my brain tumor diagnosis, surgery, and radiation treatments. For example, the night before my surgery, I thought about how most people who work out do so while listening to music. It can help motivate them to run farther, go faster, or lift more weight. I also thought about how all it takes is a little "We Will Rock You" by Queen at a sporting event to get a stadium full of people on their feet, clapping their hands, and cheering. Noting all the great reactions to it, I wondered if music could also have a positive impact on me. So I took out my smartphone and made a list of some of my favorite songs. It was everything from old school hip-hop and R&B to pop and reggae, so the sounds of artists such as LL Cool J, Timbaland, Prince, and Bob Marley filled the air as I took a shower and prepared for what lay ahead in the hours to come. I would later learn that music has the ability to help people because it can do things such as lower the stress hormone cortisol and influence the brain's "feel-good" chemical, dopamine. It has also been shown to help people who have experienced trauma by calming feelings of anxiety, reducing the perception of pain, and improving mental health.

It helps if the music is relevant to the listener, though, because *salient stimulus* can have the greatest effect. A great example of this is when I had my radiation treatments. Even though the remaining part of the mass wasn't cancerous, the thought was that the radiation could kill the cells that were too dangerous to remove. During each of my treatments, I knew that the radiation wouldn't just reach the tumor, it was going to hit whatever was in its way. At first, I felt anxious when I pictured what was going to happen to my head, but then, I thought to myself, "Okay, Jenn, you can't *not* experience this, so figure out the *how.*" Once again, music came into play. The hospital had CDs, so the radiation techs played songs for me that were upbeat. They weren't my favorites, though, so the intended effect wasn't as helpful as I would have liked. The music was from a movie soundtrack that had come out when I was in elementary school, so the songs didn't offer any nostalgic thoughts or memories for me. Thankfully, I noticed a docking station with speakers in the radiation room. Being the extrovert that I am, I asked if I could make a list of music that was *relevant to me* on my smartphone, with the thought that I could use the docking station and speakers to play the songs. Not only did the radiation techs say yes, they were in on the gig. Over the next six weeks, they would take turns getting me situated on the radiation table and fastening the radiation mask over my face. Someone would then turn on my "song of the day" before heading into the observation room to turn on the radiation. One day in particular, the song was "Rapper's Delight" by The Sugar Hill Gang. It starts out with a disco vibe, and then the rapping can be heard over the catchy tune. As the music began to play, I started to "dance on the inside" from the radiation table. It was then that the radiation tech went into the observation room. The room had a window for observing patients and a microphone for providing any additional instructions before the radiation tech turned on the radiation. All of a sudden, over the music and through the microphone, the tech said in a radio-friendly voice, "And today, we have a little radiation for the ladies." The music, the laughter, and the random act of kindness blew me away. It was almost as though I was at a nightclub and a DJ was letting people know that "radiation was on the house." Yes, my body was in the machine, but my mind was back in college dancing the night away. What happened that day also benefited the radiation tech. Having a job at a place where you know most patients and their families don't want to be there must become wearing over time. The "feel-good" chemicals of the brain could be felt by both of us, though, as we smiled and laughed when the session was done.

During one of my other radiation sessions, I listened to another upbeat song that was *relevant* to me because it reminded me of cruising around town with my friend Steve when I was back in high school. The song was "It Takes Two" by Rob Base and DJ EZ Rock. By quizzing myself on the lyrics, I forgot where I was as I got lost in the song. When the radiation machine turned off as the session ended, I was disappointed for a few seconds because I wanted to finish the song. How crazy is that? I shouldn't have wanted more radiation in my head, but I had honestly forgotten where I was. A few years later, I met someone who compared my experience to "highway hypnosis," an altered state of mind in which a person can drive a great distance in a safe and correct manner, with no recollection of consciously doing so—like driving home from the office and not remembering the trip.

The song of the day for my last radiation session was "Can't Stop the Feeling" by Justin Timberlake. As the session ended, the radiation techs and I danced around the machine to the lively song. I remember my eyes filling with tears of joy as the surgery and radiation were finally behind me—now it was time to heal.

The health benefits of music can affect children as well. Lullabies can actually lower their heart rates, reduce anxiety, and minimize their perception of pain. Music can also help them learn. For example, "The A.B.C." song is a great way for kids to memorize the letters of the alphabet. Set to the same tune as "Twinkle, Twinkle, Little Star," the music serves as a cue with its changing pitches connected by the upbeat melody. Coupled with the "chunking" of letters, the melody provides a great mnemonic device that sticks with people well into adulthood.

Music also offers health benefits later in life. One time when I was giving a speech about emotional grit at a nursing home, an elderly woman shared that she had recently sung gospel songs in her head as a way to comfort herself during an MRI. Yes, she liked the songs, but they could also serve as a *salient stimulus* because they prompted positive memories of going to church with her grandparents decades earlier.

People with dementia or Parkinson's disease can benefit, too. Music can improve mood, reduce agitation, stimulate cognitive abilities, and help facilitate motor functions. My mom witnessed this firsthand when she worked with residents of a memory-care unit. Some of the people were believed to have symptoms of Sundowner's syndrome, a condition known to increase memory loss, confusion, restlessness, irritability, and anger when the sun sets. Doctors aren't sure what exactly causes it, but there are triggers that can contribute to it, such as depression, unmet needs, disruption of the internal biological clock, infections, and low lighting as the sun sets. Reduction in daylight caused by the changing of the seasons can play a role too. The place where my mom worked was in northern Minnesota, so in December, it could be dark outside just after 4:00 p.m. Sometimes, there would be confusion between shifts because an evening nurse might talk about how aggressive or restless a resident seemed, whereas a day nurse might think, "Wow . . . that's weird. I think that resident is super calm and nice!" Wanting to get the residents to take their prescribed medications, my mom would play soothing music. As she did so, she would smile at the respective person and notice the change in their demeanor as they began to relax and take the needed medications.

There's a connection between the perception of time and memory function for people with dementia. I remember hearing stories when I was growing up about women at a local nursing home who went back to only speaking Finnish, their primary language before they had moved to the US as young adults. It was almost as though they were living in the past. I also know someone whose father had dementia, who would call her by her mother's name instead of hers. And someone I know who worked at a nursing home told me that one of the residents with compromised cognitive abilities would ask to be weighed each day because she thought she was still a flight attendant. Music can help such people by triggering thoughts and feelings of nostalgia through memories of a first kiss, attending college, or enjoying a brand-new car. The key is that the music be *relevant* to them. By allowing them to reminisce about such things, the music acts as a salient stimulus, thereby helping them with feelings of restlessness, boredom, and anxiety.

For Parkinson's disease, playing or listening to music can foster improvements in motor skills, cognitive abilities, and sensory functions by increasing the brain's production of dopamine and serotonin. That's why there are stories of people with Parkinson's disease who can dance—yet have a hard time walking.

Through my various travels, I've noticed the benefits of music being promoted at a community level. For example, I've seen airports in Charleston, Detroit, and Minneapolis with pianos and signs encouraging people to play them.

Piano at Minneapolis airport

Sign at Minneapolis airport encouraging people to play piano

I've also watched musicians perform at airports in New Orleans and Atlanta. Perhaps the most surprising place, though, was at Menards, a hardware store by my home. At the top of their escalator, there is a piano that is played for customers as they shop for things such as 2x4s, nails, and PVC pipe. Pianos can also be seen at hospitals.

Piano at Menards in a suburb of Minneapolis

I was also impressed by a library in downtown Minneapolis where a librarian told me they have a piano in a soundproof room that people can play. She said that it could be reserved for up to an hour and that people from all walks of life play there, including people who moved from houses to apartments and could no longer play in their homes. For a few summers in a row before the pandemic, I would see brightly colored pianos outside buildings in downtown Minneapolis as part of the Pianos on Parade program. Sponsored by the charitable organization Keys 4/4 Kids, the re-purposed pianos and the sheet music that people downloaded on their phones united passersby as complete strangers would stop and play tunes for themselves and each other.

"Pianos on Parade" piano in downtown Minneapolis

Music is celebrated at the community level in Sarasota, Florida, too. As part of the Sarasota Music Half Marathon, high school marching bands, along with musicians who play everything from rock and roll to dance music, play for the runners throughout the race. When I watched the runners in 2019, I met a woman who told me that her sister had just gotten out of a relationship where she lost all of her self-esteem. Running to music put confidence back in her stride as it reduced feelings of stress and helped her feel empowered again.

The novelty and tradition of "Take Me Out to the Ball Game," played during baseball's seventh-inning stretch, can unite fans, and "walk-up" songs can motivate players as they approach the plate or when a new pitcher takes the mound. Plus, as I alluded to earlier, stadium anthems at sporting events can make the fans and players go wild with the sounds of techno, rock, hip-hop, pop, and more.

It's interesting to note another way that our *favorite* moments in music can affect us physically. Scientists have discovered that before these moments, there is an "anticipatory phase" of the brain that helps predict an upcoming favorite part. This phase can trigger an increase in the "feel-good" chemical dopamine. For those of us who grew up in the 1980s, this is why it can feel good to hear the phenomenal drum solo in "In the Air Tonight" by Phil Collins. Dopamine can adapt to predictable rewards, though, and that's why we can grow tired of songs and parts of songs that we love.

Music has its own story of emotional grit. In 1984, Rick Allen, the drummer for legendary British rock band Def Leppard, was thrown from his vehicle in a car accident, causing him to lose his left arm. Rather than give up his dream, he learned to play the drums with just his right arm, using a customized drum kit that could be played by foot. With the help of Allen, the band went on to release its best-selling album *Hysteria*. Allen has also committed himself to working with war veterans who have sustained injuries like his and suffer from PTSD. By making pain his purpose, he has now helped people around the world.

Taste in music can be incredibly subjective, just like TV shows. That's why having to share a television with a stranger in a double hospital room can be a problem. You might have nothing against the TV station they chose, but if the show they want to watch isn't one of your *favorites*, it's not going to have as much meaning for you. It's also why patients appreciate when hospitals let them choose a radio station to listen to during their MRI, but it would be even better if the songs were some of their favorites. The importance, intensity, and detectability of a stimulus can make all the difference in the world. It's called "salient stimulus," and it can have a positive effect on people physically.

Music has even been known to help bring some patients out of comas.[3] Leila Neve sat by the bedside of her daughter Charlotte after Charlotte had experienced a brain hemorrhage and slipped into a coma. It had been days since the coma began, so imagine her surprise when Adele's "Rolling in the Deep" came on the radio and Charlotte began to sing along with the song that the two of them had often sung together. Charlotte then began to smile. Within two days, she could talk and get out of bed. How can music help some people awaken from a coma? According to Dr. Emery Neal Brown, Professor of Anesthesia at Mass General Hospital and Harvard Medical School and Professor of Computational Neuroscience at MIT, it is a result of salient stimulus. He thinks that she may have regained some brain functioning before the song but that it would have been too subtle to notice. The song *held meaning* for her, though, so the salient stimulus helped to wake her. There are also stories of people's beloved pets bringing them out of comas.

---

[3] Meghan Holohan, "Why does music 'wake' some coma patients?" NBC News, (June 2012), https://www.nbcnews.com/healthmain/why-does-music-wake-some-coma-patients-838063

Salient stimulus can vary by person, though. According to Dr. Javier Provencio, Director of the Neurological Critical Care Unit at Cleveland Clinic, music and tonal things are processed differently than language. That's why there are examples of stroke patients who can sing even though they can't speak.

Singing in and of itself can have health benefits. Studies suggest that it has the ability to lower the stress hormone cortisol and increase the "feel-good" chemicals endorphins and oxytocin, thereby reducing feelings of anxiety. Singing can also help people who stutter. There is still uncertainty as to why people who stutter don't do so when they sing, but it may be due to the right side of the brain being used for music, whereas the left side is used for language.

Music has also been known to provide a sense of camaraderie between astronauts and ground-support personnel, as well as between surgical teams at hospitals. It can promote cooperation between team members, lower levels of stress, and increase efficiency and a surgeon's ability to focus.

One of the most touching stories of music uniting people is that of the World War I Christmas truce. On Christmas Eve, during World War I, German troops lit up their trenches and began to sing "Silent Night" while wishing the opposing troops across the battlefield a merry Christmas. The British troops then began to sing "The First Noel" back to them. In the coming hours, scouts met in no-man's-land, gifts were exchanged, and British troops could see that the Germans had placed small Christmas trees along the protective walls of their trenches. Members of both sides then came out to greet each other. There are even accounts of a "football" or soccer game between them. The truce was short-lived, but for a moment in time, things such as music, laughter, and random acts of kindness knew no borders.

Studies show that art can have a positive effect on people as well, as it is clinically proven to reduce stress, anxiety, and rates of depression by lowering the stress hormone cortisol. It can also lower blood pressure, elevate mood, and promote healing of both the body and mind. There's even a new field of study called *neuroaesthetics*, which involves studying the neurobiological basis of the arts. Examples of forms that are studied include music, art, theatre, dance, and literature. Patients who are offered exposure to them can feel a greater sense of control in their circumstance through self-expression.

CHAPTER 9

Flipping the Script

◆ ◆ ◆

"Always turn a negative situation into a positive situation."
— Michael Jordan

When my neurosurgeon began preparing for my brain-tumor surgery, he wanted me to have (f)MRIs, during which I would lay in a machine that covered me from my head down to my thighs. While I was in the machine, a mask would be clamped over my face, and I would have a panic button in my hand to let the nurse know if I was feeling claustrophobic. I would also have an IV in my arm to deliver a dye or "contrast" into my veins for clearer images of the organs and tissues. Knowing that I have a history of passing out from needles, my dad said to pretend that the puncture wound was coming from my cat scratching me rather than a needle because that way, I would think it was cute and not worry about it. As I lay in bed at night thinking about the upcoming tests, I realized that my dad was onto something. After all, when I got my ears pierced in third grade, I didn't pass out—and that's two needles! I also thought about how I had friends in college who would pass out from shots, blood draws, and IVs, yet when we were on spring break, they got tattoos without fainting. One of the common themes I noticed was that things were better when we felt a sense of *control* because we were doing the noted items by *choice*. With that in mind, each time I had an (f)MRI, I pretended that I was at a spa getting acupuncture or Botox. I've never done either of those things before, but if I did, they would also be by choice! These were also the tests where I would sometimes pretend that I was doing them on behalf of my four-year-old nephew. In the end, I'm grateful that I never once passed out because of the IVs of contrast. When I later shared what happened with a colleague of mine, he began to laugh and said something similar had happened to him. For years, he had passed out from needles, yet the last time he had had blood drawn, he was fine. When I asked him what the secret was to his approach, he said, "I thought the nurse was smokin' hot, so I wanted to impress her." Of course, he would have done that by choice too!

Regarding the potential for claustrophobia, I asked other people ahead of time what their experiences in (f)MRI machines were like. Everyone I asked was incredibly negative. Comments included things like, "You're going to feel buried alive! You're going to feel claustrophobic even if you're not usually claustrophobic!" *Not* doing the tests wasn't an option, so I had to figure out the *how*. So each time I got into the machine, I pretended that I was back in high school in a tanning booth, which helped me realize that the enclosure of the machine wasn't the problem, it was the way I perceived it that made a huge difference. Using a tanning booth had always been by *choice* for me because it meant I was either going on vacation or going to prom. The positive experiences helped me "justify" the enclosure. By applying this mindset to the (f)MRI machine, I'm grateful to note that I never felt claustrophobic.

I later learned that this mindset is called *cognitive reframing*. It's a term used by psychologists to help people change how they view something, thereby changing how they experience it. Just like when I told the kids I was babysitting that thunder was "angels bowling"!

According to Jennifer Silvis's article titled, "Patient Centered Design: Providing the Payoff," the Children's Hospital of Pittsburgh designed rooms where children could be distracted by and participate with certain "themes" rather than fear the respective tests.[4] In doing so, they hoped to lower sedation rates. For example, in the "beach-themed" room, an oxygen tank looks like a scuba tank, the machine the patient lies on looks like a sandcastle, the walls showcase beach scenes, and music, aromatherapy, and videos also help. It's almost as though the patients are on a ride at a theme park rather than in a frightening machine at a hospital. Between 2005 and 2007, sedation rates were reduced by 99 percent. This provided benefits for the patients, caregivers (hospital staff), and family. It also benefitted the hospital itself, as with reduced sedations, the hospital could see more patients, and scans for the CT department increased 15 percent during the sample period. The liability associated with sedation was also potentially reduced.

Could this approach work for older children and adults? Yes—I didn't feel claustrophobic when I pretended the enclosure of my (f)MRI machine was a tanning booth, and I kept from passing out when I pretended needles were for Botox or acupuncture. But what if other people were encouraged to bring their smartphones to the hospital with the thought that they could download a white noise app ahead of time? The hospital would need to provide a docking station with a speaker for the phone, but the sounds of waves could help patients pretend they're resting under an umbrella at a beautiful beach or that the campfire

---

[4] Jennifer Silvis, "Patient Centered Design: Providing the Payoff," Healthcare Design Magazine, (January 2013), https://healthcaredesign-magazine.com/architecture/patient-centered-design-proving-payoff/

ambiance of frogs, crickets, and owls could make them think they're in a tent under a moonlit sky. They could also make customized lists of music like I did for my radiation treatments or even download an audiobook ahead of time. This approach, using a salient stimulus that is *relevant to the patient*, could help the person relax, dance on the inside, or get lost in a sea of positive thoughts or memories. By "flipping the script," patients can use cognitive reframing not just to get through a test but to be less apt to fear the next one. They can face their fears and build confidence along the way.

Patients can also benefit from virtual-reality simulations. I learned this when my dentist began to offer virtual-reality glasses for patients like me who were nervous to be there. Patients could choose the scene of the "adventure series" they would like to view, so I chose the ocean, which I viewed as if a scuba diver while listening to relaxing audio. By helping patients feel like they are literally someplace else, it's possible for them to actually forget they are in the dental chair. This calming effect can then reduce the perception of anxiety and pain. Virtual-reality programs are also used for burn victims as their wound dressings are changed, people suffering from addiction, and women in labor and delivery wards. The results can be amazing. I know the dental virtual-reality glasses helped keep me from getting lightheaded when the needle came my way for my cavity that day. I'm curious to see what the future holds!

CHAPTER 10

The Mystery of the Five Senses

◆ ◆ ◆

"The five senses are the ministers of the soul."
— Leonardo da Vinci

T he five senses help us interact with the world. Sight, smell, hearing, taste, and touch help us perceive our surroundings by sending messages to the brain. While much of the science is known, it's interesting to see how the five senses influence the thoughts, feelings, and behaviors of people based on their culture, experiences, or beliefs. For example, in some countries, goats' eyes are considered a delicacy, so they're served to guests of honor—whereas I can't even fathom the thought.

During economic downturns, it's common for people to talk about rising unemployment rates, falling share prices, and low consumer confidence, yet "vice stocks" tend to go up. That's because consumers are known to use things such as snack foods for comfort and enjoyment during challenging times. Depending on who you talk to, publicly traded companies such as those in the tobacco, fast food, alcohol, and gambling industries are also known as "sin stocks."

Eating foods high in fat, sugar, or salt can activate the brain's reward system, thereby triggering the "feel-good" chemical dopamine. That's why people in a bad mood tend to be drawn to unhealthy foods.

When people are feeling stressed or isolated, comfort foods can also remind them of family or friends. When I was growing up, it was a rare treat to go out to eat. Years later, the comfort foods of home became the treat as I frequently ate on the go when traveling for work. Nostalgia and novelty can play roles too. To this day, if I see a grilled cheese sandwich that is cut diagonally, it reminds me of being at my grandma's house as a kid. I swear they tasted better than normal because they were cut so "fancy"!

The five senses can also promote positive thoughts and conjure up old memories. The taste of corn on the cob reminds me of summer, and s'mores make me think of bonfires in the fall. The scent of Dove soap brings back memories of being at my great-grandma's house as a child, when we would watch bowling on TV and eat Campbell's Chicken and Stars soup.

In 2010, Minneapolis firefighter Jake LaFerriere suffered third- and fourth-degree burns in a backdraft explosion as he was fighting a house fire. Burning alive and overwhelmed with pain, he jumped two stories and landed on a porch overhang. He then used a ladder to get down the remaining story. The house had actually lifted off the foundation, and the roof blew off during the explosion. When he was being treated in a burn unit, he drew strength from children who were there healing from a tent fire. He thought, "If they can get through their treatment, so can I." Given the extreme circumstance of the backdraft, he was incredibly grateful to be alive, but he felt isolated because he craved the use of his five senses. For example, he missed listening to music, seeing friends, and touching things without the use of gloves. However, one thing that brought him joy was taste. His mom visited him regularly, so knowing that he liked cherry chocolate-chip malts, she would bring them to the burn unit for him. His parents had owned a Dairy Queen when he was growing up, so the malts gave him a sense of normalcy and a taste of home. He also remembers the distinct scent of the fresh air and cut grass as he listened to birds singing on the day he left the hospital. He felt the warmth of the sun beating down on his face, and the sky never looked so blue. All signs that he could still smell, hear, and see and that the world was waiting for him. He went on to found Firefighters for Healing with the mission of supporting burn survivors and children with options that caregivers and insurance companies may not be able to provide.

My sense of taste has always been heightened, but after my surgery and radiation treatments, it's even more intense. (I may be what's known as a "supertaster.") For example, I noticed back in college that whether I ordered a glass of water or a soft drink at a restaurant, I could always tell if the server had touched a garnishment before putting the straw in my glass. (There would normally be a subtle taste of lemon or lime on the straw.) Since my surgery, some "mild" salsas have warranted a glass of milk to subdue the burning sensation on my tongue, and some things don't taste the way they do for others. One time, I actually stopped eating an anise-flavored cookie because I thought it tasted like the scent of spaghetti sauce. My mom has a more robust palate, but she thinks that cilantro tastes like soap. The issue there is actually genetic and has to do with olfactory-receptor genes.

Since my aunt's brain-tumor surgery, she hasn't been able to taste or smell anything, but her mouth still waters if she eats salt and vinegar chips, and she can tell the difference between Coke and Diet Coke.

When I visited Montreal, Quebec, I was told about a restaurant called Onoir where customers experience food, drinks, and conversation while dining in the dark. The thought is that eating without your sight can heighten your remaining senses and help you savor the scent and taste of the food. Customers can also gain an appreciation of what it's like to not be able to see—just like the wait staff, who are all visually impaired.

Human touch can be thought of as a nice gesture, but did you know that there can also be health benefits? By decreasing the level of the stress hormone cortisol, hugs have the ability to trigger the release of oxytocin and can lower stress, high blood pressure, and risk factors for heart disease. This type of affection has also been shown to reduce pain and promote the growth of premature babies. Neonatal intensive care units can be bright, loud, and stressful for babies, so human touch can help calm them and even lower heart rates.

Weighted blankets can have a calming effect by simulating a hug and inducing a heightened sense of touch. The oxytocin released may then slow the heart rate and increase a patient's ability to rest. Warmed blankets in a hospital setting can be soothing, as can heated blankets or mattress pads in the home.

Touch can also build camaraderie, such as when athletes high-five each other or when baseball players form a "dogpile" by jumping on each other after winning a game.

Listening to music can affect us on both conscious and subconscious levels. Research has shown that shoppers in grocery stores tend to buy *more* items if they can leisurely make their way through the aisles to slow-tempo music. The *type* of music in stores can also influence buying patterns. As part of a study by the University of Leicester in England, four German wines and four French wines were displayed alongside their national flags at a British supermarket. They were similar in dryness, sweetness, and price. Researchers then studied the buying patterns of customers as traditional French or German music was played on alternate days. They found that French wine outsold the German wine when French music was played, and the opposite happened when customers heard the German music. When asked about their experience, the customers seemed unaware of the effect music had on their selection.

People tend to think of the five senses as acting independently of one another, but they are entwined as they send signals to the brain. That's why it can be hard to taste food when you have a stuffy nose. It's also why potato chips and chocolate can *taste* better when you can *hear* a distinct crunch. *Neurogastronomy* is a growing field that studies how different brain processes can affect the way we experience flavors when we eat and drink. The International Society of Neurogastronomy is hoping to help cancer patients through the modification of sound in ways that may promote flavor after a patient's sense of taste has been compromised by chemotherapy treatments.

Wanting to increase accessibility at their concerts, orchestras around the country—including those in Boston, Pittsburgh, Minneapolis, and Seattle—have hosted "sensory-friendly" performances for people of all ages and abilities, including people diagnosed with autism spectrum disorders or sensory sensitivities. The accommodations include reduced volume and lighting levels, relaxed house rules, and extra space for movement. When I was healing from surgery, I wanted minimal light in my hospital room, and even the phone ringing was too much noise. Since then, I've met people with traumatic brain injuries who need to wear sunglasses as they run errands because the lights in department stores can give them a headache. In addition, I've learned that flashing lights can trigger nausea, headaches, vomiting, and epileptic seizures in people with photosensitive epilepsy. Needless to say, the sensory-friendly concerts are a true gift.

CHAPTER 11

The Comforts of Home

◆ ◆ ◆

"There's no place like home."
— Dorothy in *The Wizard of Oz*

Feeling a sense of home is incredibly important. It's why kids get homesick at camp, adults appreciate sleeping in their own bed after a business trip, and the elderly want to pass away in their own home rather than in a public facility. It's a yearning for the familiar—a setting that's predictable and known and which thereby offers comfort and a sense of control. The more positive experiences you have at a given place, the greater the attachment and opportunity to bond with it

I remember how excited I was at camp when I would get a letter from my mom. Email and texts weren't options yet, and calling would have required the expense of long-distance charges since we didn't have access to cell phones yet. It wasn't until years later that I would learn my mom had to mail the letter the same day I hopped on the bus for camp so it would get there in time. While I enjoyed being at camp, I also appreciated having a piece of home with me.

The hospitality business also tries to provide a sense of home. That's why some hotels offer cookies at the front desk and "turn-down" service for guest rooms, where staff enters to "turn down" the linen of the bed so that it's ready for use. Some hotels even offer bedtime stories for children, coupled with easy listening music and cocktails for adults.

It's also possible to feel "at home" somewhere other than your personal dwelling. That's why realtors suggest that people bake cookies when selling their houses. The scent of the cookies, along with the cookies themselves, can help people at an open house feel *welcome* when they get there.

Years ago, I knew someone who traveled a lot for work. One day, I asked him if he missed being home. When he said no, I asked why. He said, "Because the road is my home." I didn't understand his mindset until I also began traveling around the country for work. I got to know people who worked at the Minneapolis airport by name, people in the offices I visited became friends, and I learned which airports and cities had food that I like. For example, the Miami airport had great empanadas, the Detroit airport had good lettuce wraps, Manhattan and Washington DC had delicious cupcakes, and Chicago had phenomenal pizza. The respective destinations became familiar, and the years of travel became a way of life. But what happens when being away from the familiarity of home isn't your choice?

In 1918, sparks from a train ignited a fire, and high winds fanned the flames as it swept through my hometown of Cloquet and devastated other communities. Cloquet lost hundreds of people, and thousands more were injured or displaced. According to my great-grandma, a smoky odor was in the air, but no one knew that the town was about to almost be burned to the ground. Given the fact that Cloquet is located in "lumber country," it's common to smell the scent of bonfires in the fall.

Trains were used to help people escape. Women and children went first in passenger cars, and then men followed in open railroad cars called gondolas. Within a few months of the devastating fire, people were building shacks on the backs of their lots so they could live in Cloquet again. The thought was that people would live in them until it was possible to build full-size homes again. I remember a teacher of mine sharing stories of perspective and gratitude about people who had never built their own homes before who were "grateful for the opportunity" to do so because it was a step towards a sense of normalcy. They were able to do so with the help of their neighbors.

I've also heard stories about how the northeast-Minnesota city of Hibbing had to move because there was high demand for steel, and the land under the buildings was rich with iron. It was the early 1900s, so, with the hope that people could still keep their homes and businesses, decision-makers had to think quickly. Logs were then placed under the buildings, and steel cables were used to roll them to their new locations, two miles away. However, Hibbing wasn't rebuilt to look the same as it did before, so the new town was confusing for people who had been gone for a lengthy period of time. I remember a college roommate telling me that her grandpa was deployed overseas during the move and that when he got back to Hibbing, he had to ask people where to find his family. He would joke that had he done his chores over the years without complaining, his family wouldn't have moved without him. Yes, the town had moved, but the sense of home and feelings of community needed to move too. Once known as the "Iron Capital of the World," Hibbing also became famous as the town where Robert Zimmerman, better known as Bob Dylan, was raised and went to high school before becoming a famous singer and winning a Nobel Prize.

In 2019, I visited the near-ghost town of Centralia, nestled in the foothills of northeastern Pennsylvania. In 1962, a fire spread from a landfill to seams of coal and mining tunnels beneath the town's surface. Once a close-knit mining community, it's now nearly abandoned as the fire continues to burn. Since the beginning of the fire, residents had been living with toxic gas fumes, dangerous sinkholes, and health problems. Knowing that it was cost-prohibitive to continue to fight the fire, the government bought people's homes and relocated the respective families. Some residents resisted, though, so I still saw a handful of homes. At the time of my visit, I couldn't see any smoke, but I could smell it as it seeped above ground. As I made my way through the old neighborhoods, I could see a pair of women's high-heeled shoes and children's toys scattered among the overgrown trees and tall grass. It was surreal to think that I was walking where children had once played, businesses had stood, and cars had lined the streets. Even though the town is mostly gone, the bare streets and empty lots still tell a story of days gone by—and of a fire that continues to burn.

CHAPTER 12

The Charm of Novelty

• • •

"Where there is no novelty, there can be no curiosity."
— Aphra Behn

Things that are new, different, or unique can capture our attention because the brain seeks novelty. In doing so, the "feel-good" chemical dopamine is released, which helps motivate us to pursue the perceived reward. However, once you become familiar with the stimulus, the novelty can wear off as the response decreases.

Novelty

When I was little, examples of novelty included cartoons on Bazooka Joe gum wrappers, "mystery toy surprises" at the bottom of Cracker Jack boxes, and prizes in boxes of cereal. (The key to getting one was to push up your pajama sleeve high enough so that you could shove your arm down into the cereal box to reach the coveted prize before someone else did.) When I visited New Orleans years later, I was taken aback when someone asked me if I "had the baby" in my piece of cake. Noting the surprised look on my face, I was told that the colorful dessert was called "king cake" and that it is served in honor of Mardi Gras. The tradition of the cake dates back hundreds of years, and the small plastic baby baked into the cake is meant to represent baby Jesus. Finding the baby in your piece of cake is meant to symbolize blessings and prosperity in the new year.

Novelty can be completely subjective. A couple I used to babysit for took their girls to Ireland one year. When they returned,

I asked what their favorite parts were of the trip. As the parents and eldest daughter were describing a castle, beautiful scenery, and historic sites, the little girl blurted, "Our hotel had a pool!" She reminded me of when I was little and how my mom or grandma used to take my brother and me to the Miller Hill Mall to go shopping. The mall had a huge water fountain that people would throw coins in as they made wishes, along with cool exhibits and fun stores. We didn't care, though, because we were fixated on the escalator in JCPenney. As we rode it, my mom and grandma would usually be carrying multiple bags that were probably heavy, but we would keep asking for "just one more time" because the novelty of the escalator made it so much fun. I also liked shopping with my dad because that usually meant going to a hardware store where there were tools called levels with bubbles in them.

Sometimes the new, different, and unique aspects of novelty can catch someone's eye, even when it is not ideal. One time when I was little, my parents had a friend of Dad's over for dinner. Knowing that the friend had a handlebar mustache that curled above his lips, they told me ahead of time not to stare at it. As luck would have it though, he sat across from me at dinner, so each time I took a sip of my milk, I looked at him through the bottom of my glass.

Novelty can be experienced with friends, too. I remember thinking that it was so cool that one of my friend Jen's older siblings had taught their dog to play the piano when it needed to go outside. (Jen and I both also appreciated the novelty of Michael Jackson's single white glove, but I won't confirm or deny whether or not we each wore one during our fifth-grade field trip.)

Of course, travel brings with it lots of novelty. At Seattle's Pike Place Fish Market, I saw employees in orange rubber overalls and boots call out customer orders while throwing fish behind the counter to be wrapped. They even chanted together and selected customers from the crowd to participate in the fish toss. Pike Place Fish Market now attracts visitors from around the world. I've also seen lobster ice cream in Bar Harbor, Maine; cupcake ATMs in Chicago, Illinois, and Beverly Hills, California; and mermaids and mermen swimming behind a pane of glass at the Sip 'n Dip Lounge in Great Falls, Montana. At Al Johnson's Swedish Restaurant & Butik in Door County, Wisconsin, there are goats that attract tourists because they graze on the grass roof. My favorite example of novelty at a restaurant is Gordy's High Hat in my hometown of Cloquet, Minnesota. When I worked there in high school, it opened each spring during Minnesota's fishing opener and closed with the start of deer-hunting season. The owners were snowbirds who would then head south for the winter. Known for its hand-pattied hamburgers, hand-battered Alaskan fish, homemade onion rings, and delicious malts, it has now been featured on the Food Network's *Diners, Drive-Ins and Dives.* I remember that people who were making the two-plus-hour trip from the Twin Cities to their cabins in northern Minnesota would make sure they got to Gordy's before it closed—either for the night or for the season. The business has been family-owned since 1960, and the novelty goes on to this day.

Examples of novelty in sports include the Viking helmet with braids and horns for Minnesota Vikings fans, cheese hats for Green Bay Packer fans, and the kayaks in San Francisco Bay, where fans gather for "floating tailgates" in hopes that they'll catch a "splash ball"—a home-run ball that lands in the cove. I've also enjoyed novelty at St. Paul Saints games, where I could see fans getting their haircut in the stands or watching the game from a hot tub in left field.

As I mentioned earlier, the enjoyment of novelty can be reduced over time. My dad's cousin Alan was born in London. I remember that when we visited him there, he couldn't figure out why we were so eager to see Big Ben. To him, it was just a clock tower that he had driven by for decades, whereas to us, it was something we had only seen on TV or in books, so it was a treat to see it up close and in person. I had the opposite experience in my hometown, though. Cloquet has the world's only Frank Lloyd Wright-designed gas station. While it's listed on the National Register of Historic Places, to me, it was just a place where I bought penny candy.

So how can novelty help people during times of stress? It can definitely serve as a distraction. Plus, the dopamine rush can take the edge off how you're feeling. For example, when a friend of mine's son was in the hospital, he was fascinated by the live spider someone brought in his room and loved to have a dog visit him. I also heard about a dog who would visit kids at a children's hospital with his owner. One day in particular, a mother of one of the young patients came up to the owner with tears in her eyes and said, "I owe you a huge thank you." When the owner asked why, the woman replied, "My son said he was looking forward to surgery today because that way he would get to see your dog." Wow. Novelty also helped me when I finished the last of my thirty radiation sessions. The hospital had a bell for people to ring when their radiation or chemo treatments were done. It represented a sense of accomplishment and relief. It was also a way to change the setting from a room full of strangers to a community of people supporting each other as we clapped and smiled. Novelty isn't just interesting—it's a gift.

CHAPTER 13

Attributes of Nostalgia

◆ ◆ ◆

"Nostalgia is the file that removes the rough edges
from the good old days."
— Doug Larson

Nostalgia is a sentimental longing for the past. It can be prompted by music, movies, TV shows, and other arts and the fond memories they represent. Details may fade, but the feelings carry forward. Nostalgia can help people cope with negativity because they can feel a sense of belonging from an emotional connection to the past.

Before the advent of television, it was only possible to hear people sing in person or on the radio. But in 1964, people could actually hear and *see* The Beatles, a group of four well-dressed men from Europe, on *The Ed Sullivan show*. The show was in black and white as the first in-color episode didn't air until the following week. The novelty of the group's ground-breaking music actually made fans scream and faint. When I was growing up, it was common to hear adults talk about where they were as kids when they saw the show and the ways the music rocked their world. Decades later, I saw Paul McCartney perform at an outdoor stadium in Minneapolis. As he sang "Hey Jude," I could hear thousands of people sing with him as they swayed their arms to the familiar sounds of an era gone by. The sun had set, but stage lights and the light from people's cell phones revealed tears of joy on the faces of people around me. I was witnessing the nostalgia that my dad had talked about when he had seen Paul McCartney in concert—and it was an experience that I'll never forget.

Nostalgia can also be enjoyed on social media, at class reunions, or at weddings. It's part of why DJs tailor their music selections based on the guests. It's also why at my grandma's ninetieth birthday party, my family and I watched footage of my mom and her siblings when they were little. Furthermore, it's why I purposely use my great grandma's china when I host certain holiday meals. While the place settings are beautiful, the value of nostalgia is what makes them special for my grandma, as they had been used by her mom.

The power of nostalgia is also evident in sports. In 2018, I had the privilege of visiting the Field of Dreams in Dyersville, Iowa. Originally built for a movie by the same name, it's a baseball diamond carved from cornfields after a farmer, played by Kevin Costner, hears a mysterious voice that says, "If you build it, he will come." The ghosts of great players can then be seen emerging from the stalks of corn to play ball. As I stood by the farmhouse, I pictured the ghosts playing ball in the infield and the scene where Kevin Costner's character asks a younger ghost-version of his dad, "Wanna have a catch?" As I did so, I thought about how my dad played baseball when he was growing up and the ways the game taught him the importance of patience and focus and how to celebrate victories while turning disappointments into opportunities for growth—all things he would later pay forward as he helped me face surgery and the thought that my life could change forever.

Yes, the movie is about dreams, but as I looked around the field in person, I realized that it is also about belief, faith, hope, and a zest for life—*all components of emotional grit.*

CHAPTER 14

The Impact of Smiling, Presence, and Compliments

◆ ◆ ◆

"A smile is a curve that sets everything straight."
— Phyllis Diller

Research has shown that people's need for social connections can be mirrored by their facial expressions, eye contact, body language, and tone of voice. Smiling can actually trigger the release of "feel-good" chemicals such as dopamine, serotonin, and endorphins. This is part of why people who make sales calls are encouraged to "smile and dial," because smiling can help them feel good, which in turn can influence their voice inflection and help the prospective client on the other end of the phone feel good too. It's interesting to note how during the COVID-19 pandemic, it was possible to tell if someone was smiling behind their mask because it's possible to smile with your eyes.

The need for social connectedness can have a negative effect too, though, because seeing an ex, attending a class reunion, or feeling left out of an event can cause social pain. This social rejection can activate regions of the brain that are also responsible for feelings of physical pain. These feelings can be perpetuated by social media—especially since people tend to post only positive things like pictures of a new car or the fun they're having on a trip, as opposed to sharing how they felt after a fight with their spouse or a stressful day at work. The assumption that other people are having fun without you or are living better lives is called *FOMO*, or fear of missing out. When I think of kids nowadays and FOMO, it makes me feel bad because when I was growing up, there was no social media, so I didn't know what I was missing, whereas now, kids are aware in real-time, time and time again . . . 24/7.

Studies have shown that having a social support network can promote good health. Without it, people who are lonely may have elevated levels of the stress hormone cortisol. This can then increase the risk of cardiovascular disease, weaken the immune system, and create more difficulties when recovering from health risks. Our physical, mental, and emotional health can improve when we're not alone. On one of my work trips, I met a financial advisor who would get permission from a local nursing home to sit with residents or hold their hand after they had had surgery and when they were feeling sick or lonely. He said that visiting with the person or simply sitting there without saying a word can speak volumes because it shows that you care.

When my friend Shelley was in Amsterdam for work, she was hit by a tram. After being flown back to the US, she spent weeks at a hospital trying to heal. As part of her recovery from a traumatic brain injury, she noticed that she felt uncomfortable when visitors asked her questions and wanted her to describe how she was feeling. People meant well, but she didn't want to have to make conversation with them. After five years of recovery, Shelley became certified as a volunteer at Desert Regional Medical Hospital in Palm Springs, California. As part of her visits with patients in the acute rehab department, she would introduce herself and let them know that she was recovering from a traumatic brain injury and would be happy to answer any questions. She soon realized that some of the people she was visiting would get uncomfortable if they couldn't think of any questions and wouldn't know what to say to her. Thinking about her own experience, she explained that they didn't need to ask her anything and asked if it was okay for her to just sit with them. Often the patients were returning from physical rehab sessions and just needed to rest. Her willingness to simply sit with them also benefitted their families because sometimes they needed a break. A lot of patients didn't have other visitors, though, so Shelley helped them feel supported, too. Her story is a great example of how someone's presence can be greater than their words.

Giving genuine compliments to people can enhance your own sense of wellbeing and help you seek the good in others. By initiating a positive conversation with someone, complimenting his character or a gesture he made or letting him know that you think he's a good example for others, you can set a positive tone for the room. You can also be a bright spot on someone's social media site among potential negativity.

A couple of weeks before my brain-tumor surgery, I stood with a stranger waiting for an elevator in downtown Minneapolis. As we walked inside, he asked if he could give me a compliment without me thinking he was weird. When I replied yes, he told me that he thought I had beautiful hair. After I graciously thanked him, I turned around to watch the floors of the elevator light up one by one. As I did so, my eyes began to fill with tears because I wondered if my entire head would be shaved during my surgery or if I would lose all my hair from the radiation treatments. An interesting thing then happened. The stranger said, "It's supposed to rain today."

I replied, "At least the grass will be green."

He said, "Yeah, but we'll have to mow it."

I replied, "At least it's good exercise."

He laughed and said, "I'm not going to win this conversation with you, am I?"

I turned around, smiled, and said, "Nope!" As I walked away, I could hear him continue to laugh as the doors closed behind me.

What could have been an awkward conversation put a spring in my step and dried my tears. To this day, I couldn't pick the stranger out in a crowd, but the underlying positivity of the conversation touched both of us. When I shared this story with a friend, she asked if this positive mindset comes naturally to me or if I have to put a lot of thought into it. I explained that sometimes it could take some effort, but that over time, it became a habit and then more of a mindset. She said I should research the term "neuroplasticity." She went on to explain that it is the brain's ability to be restructured and rewired as we adapt to new circumstances. What's even more fascinating is that we can encourage and stimulate it. Neurons that are frequently used have stronger connections, and those that aren't eventually die. The brain is thus able to adapt to a changing environment. There are two main types of neuroplasticity:

1. Functional plasticity: When a healthy part of the brain takes over functions from an injured part of the brain so that abilities can be restored—for example, after a stroke or traumatic brain injury.
2. Structural plasticity: The brain's ability to change its physical structure through learning. Things such as learning a new language, traveling to new places, and creating artwork can stimulate these changes in the brain.

Positive thoughts can actually help increase the number of neural connections. They can also help people process incoming data, improve cognitive abilities, and enhance creativity. On the other hand, negative thoughts can limit brain coordination, hinder creativity, and impair memory and mood.

I remember sitting in the car when I was little, as my mom pulled it around the grocery store so that one of the employees could put our bags of produce in the back of it. When he opened the door, my mom smiled at him and asked how his day was going. He stood upright and paused for a moment before saying, "Wow . . . no one ever asks me that, and that's the first smile I've had all day."

Just like my interaction with the stranger who said something nice about my hair, we can never know what someone else is going through.

Positive conversations, just like compliments, can go a long way.

CHAPTER 15

The Importance of Laughter

◆ ◆ ◆

"You don't stop laughing when you grow old, you grow old
when you stop laughing."
— George Bernard Shaw

Laughter has the ability to reduce tension, lighten someone's mood, or make someone's day, but most people don't realize that there is actual science behind it. I experienced the health benefits of laughter in a place where it took me by complete surprise: at a doctor's appointment. I was at my dermatologist's office, where I had been known to pass out from things as simple as having a mole removed. On this particular day, I needed to have a cyst removed from my arm, so as I lay on the exam table with my doctor on one side of me, his nurse was on the other, helping to keep me from fainting. As the needle was inserted into my arm, I could feel my hands get clammy, my ears start ringing, and my vision start to narrow, so I said, "You're about to lose me."

With the hope of distracting me, the doctor asked his nurse to ask me a question. So she said, "What's twelve times five?"

He responded, "No, ask her a question she knows!" As I began to laugh, the symptoms I noted went away, and they could see the color come back in my face. Toward the end of the procedure, I got queasy again while the doctor was sewing up the incision. Knowing that laughter had helped me feel better earlier, I asked how things were going. He said, "Well, I'm not going to win a quilting bee anytime soon, but I think it's fine." Too funny! Once again, my skin stopped feeling clammy and my ears stopped ringing, I stopped having tunnel vision, and the color came back into my face. At the time, it was easy to see that laughter kept me from passing out, but what we didn't know was that I had a brain tumor growing inside me—and that laughter would help me along the way.

What is it about laughter that can affect us physically? Turns out, it can lower the stress hormone cortisol and release "feel-good" chemicals such as dopamine and serotonin. It can also do things such as strengthen the immune system and improve sleep. In addition to helping people on an individual level, laughter can create social bonds by triggering the gratifying effects of endorphins. One time when I was waiting to board a flight at the Minneapolis airport, I could tell that the gate agent was new because he looked really young and nervous. The surrounding area was full of people buried in their laptops, talking on phones, or reading books, so passengers were pretty much keeping to themselves. When it was time to board, the gate agent grabbed the mic and, over the PA system, said, "Delta now welcomes any children with small parents." All of a sudden, complete strangers looked up from their laptops, made eye contact with each other, and began to laugh. The gate agent was laughing too. Even though we all came from different walks of life, the laugher created a social bond and great memories of this day.

Of course, it would be remiss of me not to mention the interactive talking gargoyle when writing about laughter at airports. His name was Greg, and when I saw him, he was located in the main terminal of Denver's airport by the luggage claim area. He would make people laugh by striking up conversations with them. As another passenger and I stood in front of him, he asked the guy if he was going to ask me out. When we began to laugh, the gargoyle then said, "Okay, fine then—I'll ask her out!"

Denver airport gargoyle

I can relate to the Minneapolis gate agent about getting words mixed up on the job. When I was in my mid-twenties, I had just bought my first house, so I worked an office job during the day and hosted at a fine dining establishment a few nights each week.

The restaurant was the place to be, so the reservation lines were always ringing, and the tables were always full. One particular evening, I had to put four or five lines on hold before I got back to the first one. When I picked up the call, I said, "Thanks for helping, *could I hold you?*"

After a pause that seemed like an eternity, the guy on the other end of the line laughed and said, "Sure. What time are you done with your shift?" Can't make this stuff up!

When traveling for work, it's common to collect funny stories from the road. Before I joined my old team, colleagues of mine were on a trip together. They audited an office during the day and met for dinner that night. Whoever had the most seniority was supposed to pick up the tab, so the team's manager gave his card to the server at the end of the meal. She was in her third trimester of pregnancy, so her ability to carry trays and run the food was especially impressive. Within minutes of receiving his card, though, she came back to the table and said, "Sorry, I'm already taken," as she handed it back. Imagine his surprise when he realized that he had given her his room key instead of his credit card by mistake. Needless to say, a good laugh was had by all, including the server. Years later, some of these coworkers visited my home when I was healing from surgery. Feeling self-conscious because of my partially shaved head, eight inches of stitches, an eye that was swollen shut, and the inability to wear makeup, I knew that I could save myself the embarrassment by not having them come over, yet I would risk feeling isolated. Or I could address the elephant in the room, laugh about it with them, move on, and feel the social ties that I craved. Thinking back to advice my dad gave me in third grade, I decided to do the latter. When I was eight years old, I was in tears because I thought the kids at school would laugh at my new glasses. My dad suggested that if they did laugh, I could laugh with them and then they would move on. I'm grateful to say that that's exactly what happened and that I learned from the experience. So when my colleagues were at my door, I remember answering it, seeing their initial expressions of polite disbelief, and having to think on my feet. Without missing a beat, I pointed to my stitches and the eye that was swollen shut and said, "If you think this is bad, you should see the other guy." The self-deprecating humor gave me a voice and a sense of control. We all laughed and then talked about other things. To this day, those guys are like brothers to me. I'll never forget what they did or how they made me feel. If such a need arose, I would do the same for them.

Laughter can help in other settings. Between staff, family, patients, or residents, it can build relationships, create bonds, reduce tension, promote dignity, and enhance coping skills. That's why "laughter yoga" is now used to serve as a distraction from the pain associated with anything from cancer to strokes and dementia. It's also used in hospice care centers.

Some of the best stories I've heard regarding laughter and the power of emotional grit are from people with brain tumors. Rather than fear what they can't see or control, they've chosen to name their tumors and joke about them. For example, one of them might say, "Steve and I went to the ballgame last night," with "Steve" being the tumor. It makes the tumor seem more friendly and the situation more manageable.

People can also watch funny movies, laugh with friends, and watch comedians online or listen to them on a streaming service. I know those things helped me when I was healing from surgery and experiencing radiation treatments. While I've always believed that laughter is the best medicine, now I know why.

CHAPTER 16

The Blessing of Pets

◆ ◆ ◆

"Dogs are not our whole life, but they make our lives whole."
— Roger Caras

When thinking about pets, it's easy to picture someone playing catch with a dog, holding a cat, or petting a rabbit. While our interactions with them can be viewed as simple "fun," the bonds that form can offer feelings of happiness and comfort while improving our mental, emotional, and physical well-being. Since not everyone considers themself to be a "pet person," the key is to be open to it. A study by the National Institute of Health found that following stressful times, people can recover faster with the help of a pet than that of friends or a member of their family due to a pet's unconditional love, loyalty, and affection. In addition, the Centers for Disease Control and Prevention (CDC) has stated that pets can reduce levels of cholesterol and triglycerides, thereby lowering the risk of heart disease in their owners. They can also help increase the chances of surviving a heart attack, lower the stress hormone cortisol, and influence "feel-good" chemicals of the brain, such as dopamine and serotonin.

These benefits and the ones described below are well-recognized, and pets are embraced at individual and community levels—now more than ever before.

• **Companionship and Comfort**

Many residential care facilities allow pets, ask volunteers to visit with their pets, and even provide robotic pets. I remember my mom telling me that when she worked at an assisted-living facility, they had a non-denominational church service each week for the people who lived there. Even though they could enjoy each other's company, residents didn't want services to start until Shatzi got there. Shatzi was a little dog who belonged to one of the residents—his name means "Little Treasure" in German and he lived up to it! I also heard about a woman with dementia at a nursing home who would sit in her wheelchair and pull herself along the railing of a hallway without speaking to anyone. People would say hi or ask her how she was doing, but she wouldn't respond. One day, a volunteer brought her cat to the nursing home for the enjoyment of the residents. As it was placed on the woman's lap, she began to pet it and smiled as she cooed, "Kitty." The mere *presence* of the cat actually reduced the effects of the dementia by lowering feelings of anxiety, loneliness, and depression. Its friendly demeanor helped the resident be more interactive. The same can be said of robotic pets. Their soft "fur" can feel real, and a wagging tail coupled with eyes that close when you pet it can help comfort someone while offering a sense of companionship. The novelty of this kind of "pet" goes a long way too—just like teddy bears for kids. In addition to providing companionship, service dogs can help people with Parkinson's disease stay balanced while walking and stand up after sitting—or even after a fall. They can also notify a family member of the fall.

Disaster-relief dogs serve as a source of comfort for students, parents, and first responders after events such as mass shootings and natural disasters. After the 2018 school shooting in Parkland, Florida, the comfort of dogs helped ease the pain. As a way to honor the dogs, each of them had its own picture in the school's yearbook. This kind of dog was also used in New York City at Ground Zero after the terrorist attacks of 9/11 to help lower the stress and blood pressure of those in need.

Businesses are starting to recognize the benefits of pets, too. Over the years, I've stayed at hotels where goldfish were provided for travelers who missed their pets at home. The novelty made people smile, and studies have shown that simply watching fish swim can help relax people by decreasing heart rates and muscle tension. I've also visited a "cat café" in Minneapolis where people can enjoy a coffee shop and lounge area that is full of rescue cats. Cat lovers worldwide have been known to enjoy cat cafés in places such as Tokyo, Japan; St. Petersburg, Russia; Madrid, Spain; and Montreal, Canada.

• Stress

In an effort to help students with the stress that can come with studying for finals, finishing homework, and writing papers, some schools have been known to provide pets. Examples include the University of Minnesota, Yale Law School, Kent State, UC Berkeley, and the University of Iowa.

There are also programs in courthouses in which dogs can do things such as accompany children during forensic interviews and help to calm witnesses and victims of crimes so they can testify on the witness stand.

At airports in Washington DC, Minneapolis, Denver, and San Francisco, I've seen volunteers with their pets help passengers who are anxious, stressed, or in need of a genuine smile feel at ease while waiting for their flight. One time in particular, I saw three guys wearing suits waiting in line to pet a golden retriever. I've also watched kids mesmerized by a little pig wearing a bowtie—they giggled while petting him.

Pig for people to pet at San Francisco airport

On one of my work trips, I met a financial advisor in Manhattan who would bring his dog to work with him. Casey, a beautiful Basenji, was a rescue dog, so after he became adjusted to his new home, the advisor decided to take him to the office when he didn't have client appointments. Other days, Casey would go to a doggie daycare rather than sit at home crated. Every once in a while, clients would stop by unannounced, and they would see Casey. Other financial advisors' clients would see him and want to meet him too. When I was there, I heard stories about clients who would purposely schedule their appointments when they knew Casey was going to be there and examples of him helping people feel less stressed when speaking about tough topics such as the death of a spouse or estate planning. I know I enjoyed being around him, too.

Casey at the office

Through my friend Mary Jo, I met a pediatric dentist in Texas who had a King Charles Cavalier Spaniel named Shortstop. The dentist knew that it was common for children to fear climbing into the dental chair, sitting under the bright lights, and listening to the loud sounds of the tools, so he wanted to help them. As a former high school science teacher, he also knew that whether it was using sports metaphors in classroom settings or asking kids about their pets when they were in the dental chair, having discussions about things that are *relevant to them* could serve as a way to connect and build trust. So, as part of his dental practice, he made a point of watching movies and studying TV shows as a way to offer more meaningfully relevant experiences for them. It's almost as though he was relating to them as a friend or peer rather than an adult in a white lab coat. When the mother of one of his patients mentioned that her King Charles Cavalier Spaniel was having puppies, the dental staff said that they would help take care of one if it could be at the office helping the children—so the dentist got Shortstop, and the rest is history.

Shortstop was kept in a tiled area by the staff's breakroom, so the patients were never sure if he was there because they couldn't see him from the lobby. Instead, they would seek him out by asking for him. Seeing him was viewed as a reward, and this rush of motivation to explore and the novelty associated with him helped give patients and their parents a dopamine rush as stress hormones subsided. Parents would even call ahead of time to see if Shortstop was going to be there because the kids wanted to bring him a toy or biscuits. These random acts of kindness also had a positive effect on the dental staff.

Parents were asked if it was okay to incentivize the kids with Shortstop. Once the dentist was given the green light, he might say to one of them, "If you lie still in the chair and are good for your appointment, you can see Shortstop!" Given the fact that pets can affect people physically, positive experiences like this not only incentivized the kids but helped them build confidence for their next visit.

Some of the children had Down syndrome or autism, so seeing their eyes brighten with excitement as they looked up from the chair was priceless. The dentist could also take pride in the fact that he was doing what he could to comfort them and that a loving dog was waiting to greet them.

Shortstop

• Social and Health Benefits

The social and health benefits of pets are nothing short of amazing. For example, I've been to libraries where volunteers bring their pets to help improve the literacy rates of children. The thought is that kids can read to the pets, knowing they won't laugh at them. This can be especially helpful for kids who are shy or those who stutter—plus, they're more apt to *want* to read, knowing they can see the pet. Attitudes toward school can be improved with this boost in the confidence of the children. Some pet shelters also have programs in which kids can read to dogs as a way to incentivize the kids to read while helping socialize the pets.

Pets are beneficial when it comes to PTSD, so some VA hospitals have them. Research shows dogs can decrease the symptoms—including the desire to self-isolate—and increase quality of life for those who are suffering. This is due in part to the companionship and unconditional love the pets can provide.

The emotional, sensory, and motor sensations that come with interactions with horses can help children with autism. Called "Equine Therapy," these interactions can provide a way for children to communicate through caring for a horse. By brushing, patting, and hugging them, the children learn to associate the care they provide with positive feelings, thereby building an emotional bridge. The benefits of this bond can then be applied to social and communication skills with people.

• Sense of Purpose, Loyalty, and Unconditional Love

Dogs can be put to work in many ways, but a few that come to mind are those who herd sheep, serve in K-9 units, act as sled dogs, or lead blind or visually impaired people as guide dogs. I also learned that in Italy, dog lifeguards assist human lifeguards. As strong swimmers that can stay calm under pressure, they are trained to jump from boats or helicopters to help rescue swimmers. Their sense of purpose and their loyalty to the cause make them invaluable partners.

Some hospitals will allow families to bring pets for loved ones who are patients. They can have a calming effect on the patient, and the family can benefit too. This picture is of someone I know who had to have surgery on her aorta because a blood clot was blocking 30 percent of her blood flow. The day brought with it lots of uncertainties, so the dog was an unexpected blessing. As I gazed at the picture, I asked, "Who held whom?"

She replied, "He held me."

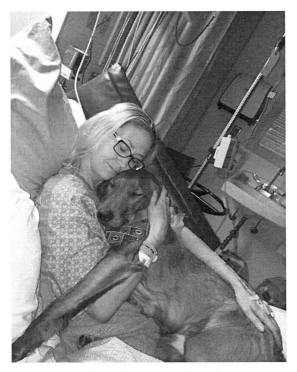

Bonding at the hospital

Another touching story came from a former colleague of mine. Before I met her, she and her girls lived at the Harriet Tubman Center in Minneapolis. The center helps women, children, and families who are struggling with relationship violence, mental-health issues, and substance abuse. Every other week, she and her girls were given the opportunity to spend an hour with either cats or dogs. When she wrote to me about the experience, she shared that the time with the pets provided a sense of normalcy for her and her family during this time of loss. The pets' eagerness to play and desire for affection also helped her and her girls feel needed during a time when they, too, were in need. The pets' welcoming demeanor and unconditional love also provided a sense of hope when she felt she had failed her children. The years have since passed, but the bonds they forged with the pets are a gift that she and her girls will never forget.

• Ways to Show You Care About Them

Given all the things that pets can do for people and the fact that so many people consider them to be family, different organizations have created ways to give back. For example, pets can now have microchips inserted so that it's easier for them to be reunited with their owners in the event that they get separated. Some veterinarians offer to euthanize pets in their homes—that way, things smell familiar to them, and there's no need for the pet to experience the dreaded car ride to the clinic.

Fundraisers such as the Animal Humane Society's Walk for Animals are a great way to show that you care. The one that I participate in each year has thousands of people raising funds by walking with their pets. I've seen large dogs wearing costumes or tutus, small dogs wearing sunglasses, little kids being pulled in wagons with their goldfish bowls or turtles, and more. The fundraising has benefits behind the scenes, but the novelty of the event catches the attention of children and adults alike.

People also come together for a service that is held annually by Minneapolis's Basilica of Saint Mary Church as part of their St. Francis Festival. It is called "Blessing of the Animals." I've heard stories of people entering the Basilica in an orderly, ceremonial manner with their pets as a way to show respect and celebrate creation. After scripture readings, prayers, and songs, there is a general blessing of the animals. Then individual blessings are performed outside after the service is done.

In addition to having a connection with your own pet, it's possible to feel good by witnessing the bond between other people and their pets. John Unger had his dog, Schoep, since he was a puppy. Later in life, Schoep developed arthritis and had a hard time sleeping, so John began to take him into Lake Superior, where the warm, buoyant water could take the weight off his joints and help Schoep fall asleep in his arms. This picture of them has touched people around the world. Within four days of photographer Hannah Stonehouse Hudson posting it to her Facebook page, it had 1.8 million views.[5]

---

[5] Christa Lawler, "Viral image sparked new career trajectory for Bayfield photographer," *Duluth News Tribune*, (July 2014), https://www.duluth-newstribune.com/lifestyle/3311456-viral-image-sparked-new-career-tra-jectory-bayfield-photographer

John Unger and Schoep by Hannah Stonehouse Hudson

These are all great reminders that pets can share in our lives and touch our hearts.

CHAPTER 17

Unsung Heroes

◆ ◆ ◆

"True heroes are those that go that extra mile for someone. That put their heart and soul into helping others. True heroes have a *heart of gold*! God bless all the heroes."

— Unknown

When people think of health scares, they tend to focus on the patient, but what about the wellbeing of the caregiver? When the caregiver is considered, it tends to be in scenarios where a parent is taking care of a child; however, it's important to remember that caregiving can also take the form of a child taking care of a parent, siblings or spouses taking care of each other, an adult taking care of a parent, or families where there is a "sandwich generation," (i.e., someone taking care of a parent and a child at the same time). Third parties can play a role, too: those that provide the direct care, protection, and supervision of children, the elderly, those who are disabled, or others in need. Some caregivers are around us even when we don't realize it, such as clergy, teachers, dentists, healthcare workers, and veterinarians.

Caregiving can be incredibly rewarding, but it can also include moral distress, compassion fatigue, and emotional labor. Examples of moral distress can be found in the healthcare industry when a physician doesn't believe that a parent's wishes are in the best interest of a child or when the decision to continue care prolongs dying—rather than improving the condition of the underlying patient. Moral distress can happen for veterinarians when clients ask them to euthanize a pet, even though the animal's condition could be treated. Or perhaps the client doesn't want a pet to be euthanized, but they can't afford the surgery that could save it. Moral distress also plays a role when a veterinarian believes that euthanasia is *best for a pet*, but the owners refuse to do so out of what feels *best for them*. As a result, the veterinarian profession has high rates of depression, substance abuse, and suicide.

Compassion fatigue is the physical and emotional exhaustion that arises from the constant demand to be compassionate and effective in helping those who are suffering. Symptoms include things such as the caregiver's poor self-care, the desire to self-isolate, feelings of irritability, and pent-up emotion. Feelings of guilt are known to arise if the caregiver thinks, "I should want to help my spouse because we made vows," or "I should be happy to help my parents because they took care of me." As a result, the temptation to self-soothe through addictions may show itself through drugs, alcohol, food, shopping, gambling, and more.

Causes of compassion fatigue may vary, but there are definitely common themes. For example, the recipient's expectations for the caregiver may be too high or the caregiver's expectations for himself may be too high. Compassion fatigue can also happen if the caregiver has the perception that everyone else's lives must be perfect because of what she sees on social media. Different cultures can play a role too. I once heard about a nurse at a nursing home who went above and beyond to connect with one of her residents. She crushed his pills and put them in jelly so they were easier to swallow, fluffed his pillow and massaged his feet, all with the hopes of getting a smile or even a *thank you*. When one of his children stopped by to visit, the nurse asked her if she had been doing something wrong. The daughter then began to laugh and shared that her dad was raised in another country where stoicism was prized and people "assumed things were fine unless they were told otherwise." At face value, it was easy to understand why the nurse thought she was doing something wrong, but that wasn't the case. Other times, the recipient may not say *thank you* because of a cognitive impairment from something like dementia or a traumatic brain injury. In addition, people may not even know how much effort or work went into something, so it may appear as though they're taking the caregiver for granted when they don't say anything. A great example of this is when a child complains about what is being served for dinner without realizing that someone had to work to buy the groceries to make the meal before it was even put on the table. Adults can complicate things, too, by not validating a caregiver's sacrifice. This can happen when the adult child of an elderly parent calls from out of state and says to the caregiver, "When I spoke with Mom, she seemed fine. What's the big deal?"

The caregiver may then be thinking, "Yes, Mom seems fine, but that's because I'm taking care of her!" The caregiver can also experience emotional labor if overwhelmed and yet feel the need to maintain a smiling face and a cheerful demeanor. Acknowledgment and expressions of gratitude can go a long way.

When I suggest to people that they write a thank-you note to their parent, pastor, teacher, dentist, healthcare worker, veterinarian, or other caregiver, they'll usually look puzzled and say, "But isn't caregiving their job?" However, people will usually understand what I'm suggesting when I equate the thank-you notes to cards they would buy for Mother's or Father's Day. Yes, these people are fulfilling their "roles," but regardless of the hat one is wearing on the outside, we're all still human on the inside.

For the first five years after my brain-tumor surgery, I had to have an annual MRI to make sure there was no evidence of any regrowth in the tissue. After the MRI was done, I would wait for a couple of hours before the nurse practitioner in my neurosurgeon's office would share the results with me. Not knowing if I would be given bad news, I chose to focus on gratitude. By bringing a blank thank-you card with me, I could write it out as I waited for the nurse to call my name. This took the focus off of me and made me feel good for wanting what was best for the nurse practitioner. Whether she had to give me bad news or someone else, I knew that her job as a caregiver had its challenges, so I wanted to express how grateful I was for her ability and willingness to be there.

Palliative care programs can also benefit caregivers. In 2019, I flew to Washington DC to participate in the National Brain Tumor Society's "Head to the Hill" event where I joined brain-tumor patients, survivors, caregivers, and other brain-tumor advocates to learn about material public-policy issues facing the brain-tumor community. We then met with congressional leaders to promote bipartisan sponsorship of the Palliative Care and Hospice Education and Training Act (PCHETA) and to raise awareness of the respective issues by personifying the needs. Through the event, I learned that palliative care and hospice care are two different things. Both provide comfort, but palliative care can begin at the time of diagnosis and continue during treatment, whereas hospice care begins after treatment has stopped and it has become clear that the person is not going to survive the illness.

Head to the Hill event, 2019

I've heard about laughter yoga, therapy pets, and music being used in both settings. The intent isn't to make light of a given illness but rather to reduce stress hormones and influence the "feel-good" chemicals of the brain for a better experience.

One of the most important things about caregiving is remembering that the needs and wants of the caregiver are important. Just like on planes during a disaster, their oxygen masks may need to be put on first so that both parties can benefit. The key is to be able to let go of some things while processing others to find a sense of balance. Showing appreciation of a caretaker's efforts can promote emotional grit along the way.

First responders and people who serve in the military can suffer from moral distress, compassion fatigue, and emotional labor. There are also stories of "vicarious trauma," where trauma is passed from trauma survivors to those who work or interact with them. This was first observed in nurses who worked with combat veterans suffering from severe PTSD. Another example is Military Chaplain Timothy Mallard, as noted in "Chaplains reunited 16 years after 9/11 attack on the Pentagon."[6] On Sept 11, 2001, Chaplain Timothy Mallard was called to the Pentagon after a hijacked plane had crashed into it and set it ablaze. The thought was that he could minister to personnel and first responders who were trying to ready the building so that search-and-rescue efforts could start. It was like a combat site where people were operating with disbelief and uncertainty about what might happen next. During one of his shifts, Mallard was told that a search-and-rescue team wouldn't go back into the Pentagon until he talked to them, so Mallard left the chaplain tent to speak to them, read scripture, and pray. By his doing that, the team felt empowered to resume their duties; however, Chaplain Mallard felt overwhelmed with grief by his duties. After putting his own needs aside and absorbing the emotional trauma of others, he questioned if he had the strength to go on.

Thinking no one could hear or see him in the chaplain tent, Chaplain Mallard fell to the ground and began to weep. Consumed by this visceral response, he didn't realize that another chaplain was nearby. Chaplain Doug Waite exuded the power of presence

---

[6] Charlsy Panzino, "Chaplains reunited 16 years after 9/11 attack on the Pentagon," ArmyTimes.com, (February 2018), https://www.armytimes.com/news/your-army/2018/02/13/chaplains-reunited-16-years-after-911-attack-on-the-pentagon/

and kindness by comforting Mallard and saying a quick prayer as he held him and let him cry. They were strangers, yet this brief encounter would not only help carry Mallard but give him the strength to help others during this sudden time of trauma, anxiety, fear, shock, and disbelief.

Sixteen years later, Mallard was able to thank Waite as part of a PBS series called *We'll Meet Again*, as hosted by Ann Curry. Their touching story serves as an example of how during times of unprecedented grief, chaplains could not only serve others but help one of their own.

When Minneapolis hosted the Super Bowl, I learned that first responders had flown in from around the country, including police chaplains. When I asked one of them how it was possible to do such a job during a time of heightened security with the potential for imminent danger, he said it's because their "desire to meet the needs of others is greater than their willingness to protect themselves."

Ready to serve

A few years later, I spoke with an officer of the NYPD whose first day on the job was 9/11. Raised in Haiti, he moved here when he was nineteen. After serving as an emergency medical technician (EMT), he became a paramedic. As part of his tenure, he worked with police on a regular basis. A number of them suggested that he become a police officer—so he started the classroom and field training on July 2, 2001. Weeks later, on September 11, 2001, he was supposed to have more classroom training as part of the six-month program. That morning, he went to police headquarters at 1 Police Plaza to get his new ID card to show that he was a member of the police academy. As he walked out of the building, the first airplane hit the World Trade Center, just a few blocks away. He had heard the sounds of the loud jet engine but hadn't known what it was. As he made the ten-minute drive back to the police academy, he turned on the radio. Radio stations had news of the plane, but any conjectures were just based on speculation. As soon as he got to the academy, he and the other recruits had to stand in formation on the muster deck for instructions. By then, the second plane had hit, and the first tower had already fallen, so just like the other recruits in his class, he was assigned a street corner with a senior officer to direct traffic. He saw a cloud of powder and smoke as he helped people who were injured cross the street but desired to walk home. The pedestrians' expressions revealed some who were incredibly grateful to be alive, others who were in a state of disbelief, and some who were sobbing.

As he worked for nearly twenty hours at East 20th Street and FDR Drive, he felt helpless because he had paramedic training, yet he was helping with traffic. He hadn't even yet finished field training for the police academy, but now, he was working in what felt like a war zone.

After sleeping less than three hours, he was tasked with blocking traffic from going within twenty to thirty blocks of Ground

Zero. He also had to escort people who were stuck north of Canal Street by walking them home to get what they needed and then leaving again. They couldn't stay because it was deemed to be a crime scene. Some of the apartments had white powder and debris in them, including remains that needed to be taken to a morgue. Most of the time, he wasn't just escorting people, he was having to be strong for them as they cried at the sight of their devastated homes—plus, no one knew when they could go home again. He was shocked and in disbelief but couldn't show it. His mom had moved to NYC from Haiti seven years before he had, so he wanted good things for her too, and he tried to find strength from within.

Between my surprising brain-tumor diagnosis, the anticipation of surgery, and the experience of the radiation treatments, there were times when I felt better *physically* while feeling a sense of hope. Not knowing why, I was grateful to learn about Jerome Groopman's book *The Anatomy of Hope*. In it, he writes about ways that research has shown a change in mindset can influence neurochemistry. The thought is that belief and expectation, two important components of hope, can obstruct pain by triggering endorphins and enkephalin peptides to imitate the effects of morphine. He also notes that hope can affect respiratory, circulatory, and motor functions.

Six months after my surgery, I sat next to someone on a plane who had served in Vietnam. When I mentioned the idea of emotional grit to him, he asked if I knew that *hope* can affect people physically. Remembering how it had helped me, I was especially curious to learn how it could affect people physically during a time of war. He shared that he had known medics who could tell the difference in the vital signs of the soldiers who were dying in their arms once those soldiers could hear the sounds of the helicopters that were coming to save them. The helicopters were called "Hueys," and their distinct sound could mean that supplies were coming, that the wounded would be rushed to hospitals, or that it may be time to go home. It was as though the people who had been waiting to die now had a reason to live.

The helicopter crews that came to save the lives of others were endangering their own. In 1963, the army began using the call sign "Dustoff" for medevac helicopter missions in Vietnam. This refers to the dust the helicopters kicked up upon landing. Perhaps the most famous of such missions was that of Dustoff pilot Charles Kelly. He and his crew risked enemy fire while trying to navigate jungle terrain during all kinds of weather and the dangers that came with nightfall. On one particular day, the enemy fire was so intense that a sergeant on the ground radioed and urged him to retreat, to which US Army Major Charles Kelly responded, "When I have your wounded." A moment later, a bullet pierced his chest, and he died at the controls. His selfless mindset of emotional grit cost him his life, but he died so that others might live because of it.

Such selfless acts can build a sense of solidarity, kinship, and community that comes with knowing someone would put your life before his or hers. The forging of these bonds can be hard to break and can take years to fade after the person gets home. My great-grandpa served in the trench warfare of World War I. When he left for Europe, his hair was red, but when he came back, it was white. Just like other troops, his unit was brought home by ship. While it took weeks to do so, the benefit was that they were able to decompress together, whereas now, individual soldiers can get home by plane the same day but may need to decompress by themselves.

While tenure in the military can provide the emotional grit that comes with living in unfamiliar states or countries, the harder part may be what soldiers experience when they get home. For example, a soldier may have a traumatic brain injury that others can't see. Or, due to advances in technology, a soldier may have survived a physical trauma that would have been deadly before, but with a diminished quality of life. Civilians might not know what to say, so there is also the concern that their inability to say anything may be perceived as indifference or that they may express *empathy* without truly being able *relate* to what happened. My college roommate, who was from Greece, would talk about how once he was done with his degree, he would go home to serve in the Greek military. When I asked him if Greek soldiers had the same problem of civilians not being able to relate to them after they served, he said no because Greek male citizens between nineteen and forty-five were required to serve. With this large military-service culture, most families had a great grandfather, grandfather, dad, brother, son, cousin, or neighbor they knew who had served—people who could relate to and appreciate the sacrifice made.

PTSD can be a direct result of being on the front lines, but it can also happen to support personnel who risk their lives. In addition, it can happen as a result of what people experience when they get home. Symptoms include things such as flashbacks, nightmares, and severe anxiety. That's why VA hospitals often have support groups and pets—to help lower cortisol levels and increase the "feel-good" chemical dopamine. It's also why I've been on flights where active service members were allowed to line up to board before general boarding could start and why I was able, like other customers, to support service members financially when purchasing things at airport stores by "rounding up at the register."

The most touching thing I've noticed in this regard was a random act of kindness that took place between two strangers on one of my flights. As I was getting situated in my seat, I saw a man wearing military fatigues get on the plane and realize that he couldn't remember which seat was his. As he looked for his boarding pass, the flight attendant offered to help. It was then that a stranger in first-class stood up and said, "Please tell him he can have my seat." My eyes filled with tears, and there was an audible gasp because the people around me were also touched. It was a great reminder that acts of kindness can benefit the recipient, anyone who witnesses the gesture, and people who learn about it later. Of course, the stranger who gave up his seat benefited too, as he could feel good for being so kind.

I've stayed at hotels that had boxes on their check-in counters for people who wanted to write a thank-you note to deployed troops, veterans, first responders, wounded heroes, or their caregivers. As part of "Operation Gratitude," a hotel guest can then put his or her note in the box for delivery to the respective recipient. Expressions of gratitude can also come from unexpected places. One of the people I interviewed for the book served as a US Marine and is now a Minnesota firefighter. In 2017, he responded to a river rescue after someone had jumped off a bridge with the intent of committing suicide. Knowing that there was imminent danger with the locks and dam of the river, he put the life of the stranger ahead of his own and saved him. One year later, the person he saved sent him a thank-you note to express his gratitude. In it, he mentioned that when he hit the water, he realized he wanted to live but didn't know how, given that he may drown. Thanks to the firefighter, he now had a second chance at life.

CHAPTER 18

The Benefits of Forgiveness

❖ ❖ ❖

"To forgive is to set a prisoner free and discover that the prisoner was you."
— Lewis B. Smedes

People tend to assume that forgiveness is a sign of weakness when in reality, it can be a sign of strength. Just like acts of kindness, both the person who decides to forgive and the recipient of that forgiveness can benefit. Unconditionally forgiving someone can literally improve your physical, mental, and emotional wellbeing. For example, it can reduce pain, decrease blood pressure, improve sleep, and lower the stress hormone cortisol— whereas anger, hostility, or holding a grudge can increase stress hormones and promote poor health. These are important things to keep in mind about the hurts that people carry and the grudges they hold.

Forgiveness can also be needed at a community level. In the mid 2000s, my dad learned about a trip to Vietnam where he could volunteer to distribute restored wheelchairs and other mobility aids to people in need. He had served in Vietnam during the war, and he also knew that the trip would be a great opportunity to see how things had changed over the last few decades. The trip was spearheaded by someone he knew who was married to the then-mayor of his town in Wisconsin. For years, she had served as a high-profile advocate for people with disabilities, as she herself had become wheelchair-bound in the 1990s from an adverse reaction to anesthetics that were given to her during a dental appointment. Her tragic story helped draw attention to the cause as she served on the Mayor's Commission on Disabilities and with other organizations.

While in Vietnam, my dad saw firsthand her ability to deliver a message of hope to adults and children alike as they received the medical equipment they needed. He also had an opportunity to help her when she was unable to use her chair. The trip was a success. Many people were touched, including the volunteers.

Imagine their surprise when they later learned that not all was as it seemed. Over the past few years, the woman had secretly been regaining the ability to walk. This was discovered when her daughter came home unexpectedly and saw her walking. Their family was in shock and disbelief, as was their church community. When the story hit the local news, there were stories of how people had helped with everything from making her home more handicap accessible to supporting her various causes because they believed in her and what she represented. *Forgiveness was key as it helped people heal.*

CHAPTER 19

The Multiple Facets of Grief

◆ ◆ ◆

"Don't cry because it's over. Smile because it happened."
— Dr. Seuss

As part of my research for this book, I interviewed people about their stories of emotional grit. Often, they expressed a sense of loss and of feeling misunderstood, as well as a strong sense of perseverance. I learned that there's a difference between *grieving* and *mourning*. *Grieving* is the deep sorrow that can be felt on the inside, whereas *mourning* is the expression of grief on the outside. If someone isn't very expressive, it's easy to assume they're okay. Still waters can run deep, so it's important to ask how someone is feeling. People may want to express their grief but feel like they can't. I met a guy who had a traumatic brain injury from a motorcycle accident. Because people viewed him as a "tough guy" on the outside, they would say things to him like, "You're so tough!" or "You're going to be fine!" While the words were meant to be a compliment, they actually made him feel like he was being held to a higher standard that limited his ability to express his feelings of vulnerability and grief for the life he once knew.

There are two different types of grief:

1. *Anticipatory grief* is feeling the pain of loss while someone is still living. Examples include things such as anxiety, sadness, or dread when a loved one is suffering from a long-term or incurable illness. Just "knowing what is coming" can make people yearn for life as it once was—and a sense of normalcy.

2. *Ambiguous grief/loss* can show itself in different ways. For example, it can be feelings of loss when a loved one is here *physically* but not present *psychologically*. Mental illness, dementia, forms of addiction, and brain injuries can be causes of this kind of grief.

Ambiguous grief can also represent as feelings of loss associated with a loved one who is physically absent but psychologically present. It is something that can happen when experiencing a breakup or divorce, separating from someone during a natural disaster, finding out that a loved one has become "missing in action" during a time of war, or knowing that someone you love has been kidnapped. When the terrorist acts of 9/11 happened, social media wasn't popular yet, so it was common for people to print "Missing" posters displaying pictures of their loved ones and place them on lamp posts, telephone poles, bulletin boards, and hospital walls with the hopes that someone would happen to see one and let them know if the people on that poster were alive, injured, or deceased.

In the late 1970s and early 1980s, there was no uniform system to raise awareness about missing children. It would be years before the AMBER Alert system would be put in place and GPS tracking would be an option. Wanting to help the cause, a dairy farm began to print milk cartons with pictures of two local paperboys who had been kidnapped. Other dairy farms began to follow suit. For years, pictures of missing children could be seen on the sides of the cartons produced by various milk-packaging companies.

With ambiguous grief, there's nothing tangible like a funeral or burial to promote closure and the ability to move forward. From lamp posts to milk cartons, though, it's inspiring to see how people who lacked control of a situation tried to make up for it with creativity.

When my ex-husband, Scott, was growing up, his dad was a traveling architect, so he didn't see him very often. When his dad was home, he was distant and emotionally removed, so Scott doesn't have many fond memories with him. His dad was 6'4" and devastatingly handsome, but he knew it. Scott's mom was a runner-up for Miss Universe, so from the outside, people assumed that they were a perfect couple who had it all. His dad's heavy drinking and quick temper told a different story. Wanting to keep up the façade, Scott tried to maintain a low profile and some privacy for the family. One morning, he woke up to find his dad's car parked in the middle of the lawn, so as he waited for the bus, he tried to cover for his dad by telling other kids that the brakes were broken. His parents divorced when he was twelve, so Scott had very little contact with his dad in the years that followed. They went on to talk about every six months or so, and Scott agreed to help take care of his dad. He knew that it wouldn't be easy, but he believed that it was the right thing to do. There was a surreal dichotomy between his dad's inability to bond with him and his continued desire for his dad's approval. When his dad passed away, Scott wasn't just mourning the loss of the *father* he had—he was grieving the death of the *dad* he never knew.

Years ago, I heard a sermon about grief. In it, the pastor used the term *widow* for a woman whose spouse passed away, *widower* for a man whose spouse died, and *orphan* for a child who lost both parents. He went on to say that there's no specific term in the

English language for a parent who has outlived one of their children. That's because children aren't supposed to go first. The night before my brain-tumor surgery, I chose to go through my burial wishes and healthcare directive with my Mom, Dad, and Dad's wife. They hadn't asked me to do so, but out of respect for them, I wanted to broach the ominous topics. We had been told that the surgery may cause a blood clot, stroke, blindness, or even death. Percentage-wise, the risks varied, but I knew their lives would change if I didn't make it through surgery. I also sat down a couple of times to write them thank-you letters, with the thought that a friend of mine could deliver them if needed. Each time I tried to write, though, I was afraid of leaving something out, so rather than get bogged down in the details, I asked my friend to thank them on my behalf if I passed away. Upon reading this book, they will learn for the first time about what happened behind the scenes.

The fortitude that can accompany grief is an amazing thing. At the funeral for the son of one of my grandma's friends who had passed away, people asked her how she was coping with the loss. He had been in his twenties and had died way too young in a drunk-driving accident. Rather than feel consumed by the years that had been *lost*, she said that she was grateful to have had him for *as long as she did*. Her incredible mindset of emotional grit continues to inspire strength in others to this day.

What are some things third parties can do to help? Sometimes it's simply admitting to someone that you want to help, but you're not sure what to say. You could also mark your calendar for the one-year anniversary of someone's passing so that you can reach out to their loved ones long after other people's lives have gotten back to normal. Or it could be doing a random act of kindness for them. Pets can certainly help. Some funeral homes now keep pets to help grieving family members and funeral attendees lower stress hormones and increase dopamine so that they can feel a sense of comfort when visiting the home and at the service.

CHAPTER 20

The Draw of Athletics

◆ ◆ ◆

"It's not whether you get knocked down, it's whether
you get up."
— Vince Lombardi

Emotional grit is incredibly evident in sports. From the discipline it takes to "play through the pain" to the psychology of playing heavily favored opponents, athletes live and breathe Friedrich Nietzsche's famous quote: "That which does not kill us makes us stronger."

The neuroscience of games can be felt by players and fans alike. While *playing* certain sports can cause an adrenaline rush, *cheering* for them can create a sense of belonging that helps fans escape the responsibilities of everyday life. That's why people will yell at the TV or make comments like, "*We're* down by five." When your team has the lead or has just won the game, the body can produce the "feel-good" chemical dopamine, and when your team does poorly, the brain can produce cortisol as a sign of stress.

I used to fly to Green Bay, Wisconsin, for work, so I witnessed how loyal fans could be in the cold. Person after person would tell me that shoveling snow off the stands at Lambeau Field was an honor, so they did so without expecting to get paid. And once pay was available, there was a problem with people not cashing the checks because they represented the sense of purpose and social connectedness that came with supporting the team. I also heard stories about how hard it was to get season tickets because fans would inherit them from their families.

One time, I went to a game at Lambeau Field because my boyfriend at the time was a huge Packers fan. A band was playing at a pre-party event in the tent of a nearby steakhouse. It was freezing outside, so I wasn't surprised to see the breath of the singer in the cold air, the cutoff gloves of the keyboardist, and the scores of fans wearing bright orange or camouflaged hunting gear to stay warm. The camaraderie in the cold reminded me of watching hockey games in high school, so to me, this environment was normal. I could tell this was normal for other people as well because rather than talk about the temperature, they were more concerned about who had the best cheese hat. Ah, the power of perspective and novelty. The Packers came from behind that day—and the unexpected win could literally be *felt* by all.

CHAPTER 21

Ten Standalone Stories of Emotional Grit

◆ ◆ ◆

Miracle on Ice

In 1979, the nation was still reeling from feuding beliefs about the Vietnam war, the resignation of President Nixon, and long lines at the gas pump—and we watched in disbelief as inflation soared. The Iran hostage crisis further crippled the nation as people began to question who we were and where we were going as a country. There was also tension in the air because stakes were high between the US and the Soviet Union. It was the era of the Cold War, and Russia's neighboring countries had been annexed to form the Soviet Union while others in eastern Europe fell behind the Iron Curtain as well. It was East vs. West and Communism vs. Capitalism—people lived under the threat of nuclear war and craved a sense of hope. Little did they know that it would come in the form of college-aged kids playing a game of hockey that would later be known as the greatest moment in American sports history.

One such player was Rob McClanahan. Having grown up in North Oaks, Minnesota, he had played hockey since he was six years old, and he continued to do so while attending Mounds View High School. He went on to play for Herb Brooks at the University of Minnesota, where they won the NCAA Division I National Championship. Brooks was asked to coach the 1980 US Olympic hockey team, so McClanahan and a number of his teammates joined him in Colorado Springs, Colorado, where they moved into dormitories and tried out for the team. Of the eighty-four players who vied to play for Brooks, twenty-six made the cut, with the caveat that six additional people would need to be cut before the end of the year. The remaining twenty would then go to the Olympics in Lake Placid, New York, where they would play other countries (including three that no longer exist).

Throughout this time, the players participated in over sixty exhibition games against college teams, top minor league teams, and four National Hockey League teams. They weren't just playing the other teams—because they were also competing with each other. Since Brooks knew that they came from different schools where they were used to being adversaries, he focused on getting them to think as a *team* rather than as a group of individual players. That's why he would say that the name on the front of their jerseys (USA) was more important than the one on the back (their names). Throughout the season, he brought in three additional players who had already tried out for the team to join the current ones as they played in a series of games. He did so because he said he wasn't comfortable with the current line-up. After a game in Milwaukee, a few of the original players approached Brooks because they didn't like having the "outsiders" join them on the ice. The thought was that it didn't seem fair, especially since the rest of them had been working so hard together all season. Brooks got what he wanted. Yes, their talent helped get them there, but their newfound feelings of solidarity would also help carry them forward. Once all the cuts were made, the twenty remaining players, including

McClanahan, knew they had made the team. But what they didn't know was that *they were about to make history.*

One of the reasons they succeeded is because at their first practice after tryouts, Brooks said, "We may not be the most talented team, but we're going to be the best-conditioned team." When you're in the best shape, your mental toughness and stability are that much greater. This mindset was evidenced when players who were completely exhausted at the end of their shifts could still stay on the ice to make the plays. Focusing on the things that they could *control* rather than concentrating on the things that they couldn't, they followed a disciplined approach—and it fueled them. The players practiced in a way that allowed them to access deep reserves of conditioning and technique when they were in the most important moments of the season.

Brooks was a pioneer in his willingness to acknowledge both the need for conditioning and the psychological aspects of the game. By pushing the players beyond their physical and psychological limits, he could make them realize that they were capable of far more than they imagined. However, he also knew that a team is only as good as its weakest link, so he wanted the best players to embrace the weakest ones—that way, they could all play a role together. Brooks wasn't setting up people to fail; he was exposing them to different situations in which they could find success. When players missed passes or body checks, Brooks knew that they could *learn from it.* Yes, Brooks was tough, but when asked if he would play for him again, McClanahan said he would do it again tomorrow.

Brooks wanted to use this innovative approach even though it was far different from what was used with prior US Olympic teams. Unlike the traditional North American style of coaching, the defensive line was as involved on the offense as the forwards were. By giving them such freedoms, Brooks opened their minds to the possibility of using creativity when playing the game. This was different from his more structured style of coaching at the University of Minnesota, but he was a student of the game. By learning from the European style of hockey, the team had a better chance to compete with them.

The team played their last exhibition game right before the Olympics began, on February 9, 1980. It was at Madison Square Garden against the mighty team from the Soviet Union known as the Red Army. From 1963 through 1972, they had won nine world championships and three Olympic gold medals. They won their fourth straight gold in 1976 and reclaimed the world championships in 1978 and 1979. On top of that, their goalie, Vladislav Tretiak, was deemed to be the best in the world. Their team wasn't just known—it was feared. The Americans were young amateurs who had played together for a matter of months, whereas the Soviets were professionals who had played together for years. It was David vs. Goliath, and Goliath won that day 10–3.

In 1946, Vasily Stalin, son of the Communist leader Joseph Stalin, served as the head of the Soviet Union's sports programs and called for the creation of the nation's first-ever Canadian-style ice-hockey teams. Anatoly Tarasov was one of those who was tasked with learning how to play ice hockey, but he had limited means to do so. He had never actually seen a game before, so he had to *figure out the "how."* By observing other professions, he was able to use unorthodox methods to create exercises for the players. For example, he would use the mental strategy of chess and the physicality of ballet to increase the mental acuity of the players and the dexterity of their moves. Players performed somersaults and pirouettes wearing skates and heavy pads. His innovations established the country as a dominant force in international competitions and garnered him a place in history as the "Father of Russian Hockey." All of the players were under twenty-five-year contracts as soldiers of the Soviet army, and in 1977, Viktor Tikhonov began to coach the team. His domineering style was more academic than Tarasov's because it was driven by data. He held practice for as many as eleven months out of the year and frequently required players to sleep in military barracks so that they were away from their families and friends—as their focus was to be on the sport. Going into the 1980 Olympic games, they weren't just favored to win, it was assumed, as part of their global domination.

The day before the opening ceremonies, Team USA tied Sweden 2–2. They then beat Czechoslovakia 7–3, Norway 5–1, and Romania 7–2 before beating West Germany 4–2, which set up a semifinal against the Soviet Union. Meanwhile, the Soviets annihilated teams such as Japan (16–0) and the Netherlands (17–4). The game between the Soviet Union and the United States was viewed as predator vs. prey, and the world watched with bated breath to see who would be left standing. It would also serve as a proxy for Cold War conflict and ideologies that stood their ground off the ice as well.

Fans from all over the United States paid to have telegrams sent to the team wishing them good luck. They were displayed on the walls of the locker room and the corridor to the ice. Fans in the street and inside the packed arena chanted "U-S-A!" As part of his locker-room speech to the team, Brooks told the players that they were born to play hockey and were meant to be there. The plan was to beat the Soviets at their own game. Because the Soviets were so well-conditioned and so fast, most opponents knew that they couldn't outskate them, so after ten minutes or so, they would try to defend rather than attack. However, Brooks's strategy had been to have the best-conditioned team so that they didn't need to defend. That way, they could just attack throughout the game.

As the players made their way down the hall and onto the ice, they could hear the hum of the crowd as the chanting got even louder: "U-S-A! U-S-A!"

In the first period, the Soviets scored first. Then Buzz Schneider scored for the US. The Soviets scored again, and with one second left in the first period, Mark Johnson scored, tying the game 2–2. The fans cheered and waved American flags as they now knew anything was possible.

Tikhonov was frustrated though with the goal, so he surprised both teams by replacing goaltender Vladislav Tretiak with Vladimir Myshkin. In the second period and beginning of the third, the Soviets dominated the game and scored, making it 3–2. With twelve minutes left, Mark Johnson tied the game again. The crowd went wild. Flags continued to wave in the air. Later, people swore that the building had actually vibrated from the loud cheers that day in Lake Placid. With ten minutes to go, Mike Eruzione scored and gave the nation a continued sense of hope. The score was 4–3. The players still needed to be in attack mode as they ran down the clock. With just seconds to go, ABC sportscaster Al Michaels said in part, "Twenty-eight seconds . . . the crowd going insane . . . Kharlamov shooting into the American end again . . . McClanahan is there . . . the puck is still loose . . . eleven seconds! You've got ten seconds! Countdown going on right now! . . . Morrow up to Silk . . . Five seconds left in the game! . . DO YOU BELIEVE IN MIRACLES?! YES!"

The players were overtaken by euphoria as the team rushed towards one another, raised their arms in victory, jumped on the ice, and heard the fans roar. Afterward, they ascended into a sea of high fives and sang "God Bless America" as they celebrated the win they had never seen coming. The Soviets had outshot them 39-16, yet they had come from behind three times. The underdog was now the top dog, and even President Carter wanted to celebrate, calling Brooks to congratulate them.

The team had done the hard part, but there was still work to do, as they would now play Finland, two days later, for the gold. On February 24, 1980, the US secured the gold with a winning goal from McClanahan and a final score of 4–2 over Finland. As the American flag was elevated during the national anthem, the players felt an immense sense of pride. They were no longer college-aged kids who played for different schools; they were a united team who played for their country. The very next day, they would celebrate their victory with President Carter at the White House.

While the years have passed since this remarkable feat, the lessons learned are still relevant today. Discipline. Drive. Commitment to sacrifice. And a willingness to persevere in pursuit of an unknown. All attributes of the twenty young men who beat the Soviets, won the gold, and inspired the nation. Brooks passed away in 2003, but his legacy lives on through the players and fans who apply these principles both on and off the ice—making it possible to not only pursue miracles but to believe in them.

Band of Brothers: Bear Attack

In the fall of 2018, Brad Johnson, Justin Reid, Todd Green, and Tom Therrien headed out on a camping trip in the Beartooth Mountains of Wyoming. The group had hiked there before, but this was the first time that Todd had joined them. It was his job to pack a tarp that could blend into their surroundings; however, he brought one that was white. The other guys teased him about the tarp and the large, heavy camera case that he wanted to bring on the eight-mile hike along with their sixty-pound backpacks. Little did they know that these items of fodder would serve a higher purpose in the hours to come.

The narrow hiking trail cut through dense forest and rugged terrain. With just a half-mile to go, Brad grabbed Todd's camera case and began to hike ahead of the group. After he got about one hundred yards out of their sight, he heard a rustling in the woods about thirty feet from him. It was two charging grizzly bears who were closing in on him in a matter of seconds. There wasn't enough time to remove the safety clip from his bear spray to use it—so he threw it at one of the bears and missed. He then turned his back towards them, and the bear attack landed him on his stomach. The bear or bears were then immediately on him, sniffing and clawing at his overstuffed pack.

The pain was excruciating as one of them bit through the muscles of his right shoulder. Brad then released a high-pitched scream as the bear's teeth crunched through his shoulder blade and broke it. At that time, the bears repositioned themselves. He initially thought they were sitting on top of him, but they were probably standing on him with their front legs moving around as they continued to paw at his backpack. It was then that he could feel teeth sinking into his left shoulder, so he let out another high-pitched scream as he felt muscles being torn from his shoulder and teeth sliding down his left arm as they ripped off the majority of his tricep and made their way into the bone. The bears also broke his elbow and left a large hole in the back of his arm that exposed bone.

Not realizing that the bears had decided to leave, he continued to lay face down and wonder what was going to happen next. Was he going to die? He began to think of his family. Knowing that he may never be able to hold them again, attend weddings, enjoy grandkids, or grow old with his wife, he began to pray.

As the others were crossing a dry creek bed, Tom said, "Hey, did you guys hear that? It sounds like an eagle or a hawk screeching." It didn't sound human at all—but it was Brad screaming.

They thought that Brad had come across something feeding that was making the "animal" noise. The third time they heard it, there was enough human voice in the scream to be recognizable, so Justin took off running. He almost ran past Brad because the bears had thrown him behind a log. He was lying on his right side, drenched in blood.

When Tom and Todd got there, Brad kept telling everyone that he believed he had an arterial bleed and that they should leave him to save themselves. He asked Tom to get out his phone to make a video of what he believed would be his last words to his family.

Relying on his training as a Minneapolis fire captain, Justin assessed their surroundings and noted that they were four hours into the woods with no cell signal. As he began to pray and pack Brad's wounds with gauze bandages, Tom and Todd cut down trees to make a stretcher with parachute cords. Unfortunately, the makeshift stretcher wasn't going to work as it was too hard for Brad to lay on it with his wounds. Because of Justin's medical training, it was decided that he would stay with Brad as Todd and Tom made their way through the wilderness to find help. During their hour-plus run, Todd blew a whistle until they came across two hikers who knew the area well and were willing to race ahead of them to notify authorities.

While they were gone, Justin was able to get Brad to walk to a sparsely wooded area that backed up to a rock formation where they could set up camp. As they would later learn from a game warden, the bears probably hadn't gone very far from the attack site because of the food source there, including the contents of their backpacks. Justin knew that he needed supplies for Brad, so he instinctively grabbed his bear spray and went back to the attack site four or five times to get water, sleeping bags, food, and other supplies. The oversized camera case that Brad had been carrying earlier that day had been destroyed by the bears, so what was once considered to be an unnecessary accessory was now viewed as a blessing because the respective claw marks could have caused extensive injuries.

The white tarp ended up being useful as well, because it was used with smoke to signal a helicopter. Involved in another rescue effort at the same time, the helicopter only had room for Brad. As he was airlifted in its rescue basket, Justin could hear the blades of the helicopter cut through the evening sky. As they did so, his heart was filled with emotion. Not because *he* was being left behind, but because it was filled with gratitude as he knew *Brad* was going to live.

One of the onboard nurses told Justin that approximately three hours later, a search party would come for him by foot rather than by helicopter because it would be dark outside. She gave him a jacket, a sleeping bag, and a satellite phone. After gathering firewood by the light of his cellphone, Justin lay under the stars and reflected on all that had happened. As he began to feel drowsy, he didn't hear the five people approaching who had come to save him, but he did hear one call out his name. When he looked up, he could see the five headlamps of a game warden, a federal agent, and three volunteers who had just hiked for six miles in the dead of night to rescue him. The selfless acts of the strangers overwhelmed him with gratitude as he thought about their sacrifice. This time he wasn't the first responder—he was the one being saved.

When he was able to reunite with Brad, Tom, and Todd the next day, everyone knew it was a trip they would never forget. After all, they went on the trip as friends but came home as brothers. One life saved and four changed for life—forever bound by a story of loyalty, faith, gratitude, and grit—great reminders that the best things in life . . . are free.

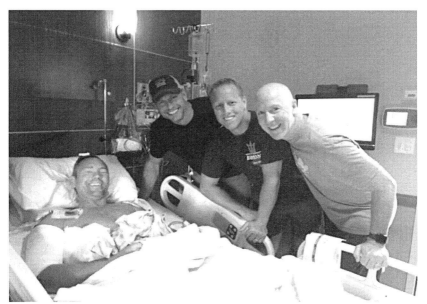
Brad Johnson, Justin Reid, Tom Therrien, and Todd Green

A Mother's Love

Dayna (Sylvester) Bottila doesn't remember being told she was adopted...she just always knew. Her struggle centered on feelings of abandonment and questions about her identity. Noting that she didn't look like anyone in her family, she felt "less than" and wondered if they would abandon her too.

Her grandma Mayme would help her feel better by telling her that she was special and that she should view her adoption as being *chosen*. The kind words helped Dayna feel accepted and loved.

At times, she still felt alone. She didn't say anything to anyone because she didn't want her family to feel bad. Thinking that her birthmother had placed her for adoption because she was an "inconvenience," she told herself that she would "never do that to a child" because the feelings of "not belonging" were unbearable.

Sometimes, at a doctor's appointment, she would be asked about her family's medical history. When she would tell the physician that she didn't know anything because she was adopted, the doctor would say, "I'm sorry," as if being adopted should have a stigma with it.

Collectively, moments like these weighed on her heart, so she acted out as a teenager by occasionally not making the best choices. At the age of sixteen, Dayna's life took a turn when she had an unplanned pregnancy herself. She was terrified, and she hid the pregnancy for months as she and her boyfriend considered their options.

After weighing the circumstance, not just in her head but also in her heart, she decided that she couldn't be what was best for her child. She loved him but felt that that wouldn't be enough, as she wanted him to have more than what she could offer.

Although the mere thought of this decision was more than she could bear, she realized it wasn't about her, it was about him, as her love for her son was greater than her love for herself. This selfless mindset not only helped her with her son's adoption, it helped her with her own.

After all, her grandma Mayme was right—Dayna's son was not only adopted by a family, he was *chosen* . . . just like his mom.

The Collapse of the 35W Bridge

In 2007, Garrett Ebling was making his way home after enjoying happy hour with colleagues in Roseville, Minnesota. He was north of Minneapolis and needed to drive south on Interstate 35W to reach the western suburb of Minnetonka. As he approached a bridge that stretched 1,907 feet over the Mississippi River, he experienced stop-and-go rush hour traffic and needed to navigate construction on the hot summer day. He was driving a Ford Focus hatchback with the windows down, listening to upbeat music to celebrate the fun he had with his colleagues. The bridge was four lanes wide, north and south—and 110 feet above the water.

About a third of the way over it, he noticed that random sets of brake lights all of a sudden became a sea of orange—and then he watched as the cars in front of him disappeared. His initial reaction was that of shock and relief because he had just seen something happen, yet he was okay. Just then, the part of the bridge that was beneath him began to nosedive into the river below. It was as though everything was happening in slow motion as he heard the sounds of the city, traffic, and whatever was happening around him. He locked his arms on the steering wheel, slammed on the brakes, and said to himself, "Ride it out, ride it out, ride it out!!" The car slid forward and dove into the water below, which was already littered with debris.

He doesn't remember anything else that day, but was later told that he had regained consciousness. The entire front of the car was submerged, and when two good samaritans found him, the water was already up to his collar bone. They could see that his left leg was outside the car and that his face was covered in blood.

One good samaritan was a dental student from the University of Minnesota who was moving into his apartment that day across the interstate from the bridge. The other one was a man from Wisconsin who had been driving alongside the river when he saw the bridge collapse. He knew that river currents could be dangerous, but on that day, he could also see that cars, steel beams, exposed rebar, chunks of concrete, and jagged debris might slice, pin, or trap someone . . . including him. Knowing that he couldn't help anyone if he couldn't stay safe, he had to make a split-second decision—not whether he *wanted* to save someone, but *who*.

Thankfully, Garrett was located in a place where the good samaritans could safely reach him. Garrett would later learn that his car had collided with another one midair before crashing into the water below. His seatbelt was jammed, so the man from Wisconsin went back to his truck and got something to cut it. The two good samaritans then pulled him through his driver's side window. One of them floated on the water and served as a "raft." The other laid Garrett on top of him and pulled them to shore.

Within thirty minutes of the bridge collapse, Garrett was on an operating table in Minneapolis. His injuries included a severed colon, one broken ankle and another shattered, a ruptured diaphragm, a collapsed lung, shattered vertebrae, optic nerve damage, a traumatic brain injury, a shattered arm, missing teeth, and all of his facial plates were shattered as well. His mom would later need to provide a picture of him, so that surgeons could reconstruct his face.

The day of the accident, his friends and family didn't even know where he was because his cell phone was at the bottom of the river. His mom and grandparents learned about the bridge collapse when they saw it on the news. Wondering if Garrett was part of it, they called hospitals—but to no avail. His roommate noticed that he didn't come home that night, so he also became concerned. Hours later, at 4:00 a.m., he saw news footage of a man being taken out of an ambulance who was wearing a shirt that looked like one of Garrett's. Fearing that it was him, he called Garrett's boss and asked what he had been wearing the day before. That morning, he and Garrett's family finally learned where to find him.

Three weeks into his hospital stay, Garrett woke up, but he didn't know where he was. As his mom informed him about the bridge collapse and assured him that everything was going to be fine, he could tell that his right eye was closed, his jaw was wired shut, he had a tracheal tube down his throat, his left foot and one of his arms were in casts, he was attached to IVs, and machines were beeping all around him. He would be in the hospital for roughly two months before relearning how to do things such as chew, swallow, and walk again. He lost his sense of smell, and his sense of taste was compromised. For example, he can "sense" when there is smoke from a campfire or cigarette, but he can't smell it.

The physical healing was easier than healing emotionally because physically, there were things that he could do with tangible results. Wanting to get back what the bridge had taken from him, he set goals for himself and "put in the work" to make things happen. While he has made an immense amount of progress, some things have settled into a "new normal." For example, his sense of balance is now impaired, and his ability to articulate his thoughts has been compromised.

Not wanting the bridge to "win," he decided to fight back by facing his fears. Within two years of the bridge collapse, he began to ride a motorcycle and went skydiving for the first time. He felt especially empowered when skydiving because it allowed him to give up control *by choice*, whereas the bridge had stolen that ability from him before. The anticipation of the jump made him feel nervous as the plane began to ascend thousands of feet in the air. However, once he left the plane, the freefall at 120–140 mph made him laugh as he faced his fears and won.

Yes, the *bridge* had fallen, but *he* became stronger because of it. His zest for life helped him cheat death by not only surviving his injuries but learning to truly live because of them.

Caregiving and the Heavyweight Champion of the World

When Donna Gagne reflects on her youth, she remembers learning that her dad excelled in both high school wrestling and football. She also remembers hearing stories about how during World War II, he had joined the marine corps and had been asked to teach wrestling moves to soldiers as self-defense techniques for hand-to-hand combat. During his successful tenure at the University of Minnesota, he had played football with Bud Grant, another phenomenal player, who later became the famed head coach of the Minnesota Vikings. Her dad had wrestled in college as well and had qualified to become a member of the 1948 Olympic wrestling team. In addition, Donna remembers hearing stories about how her dad had been drafted by the Chicago Bears but had decided to pursue professional wrestling instead as it had paid better at the time. As an amateur and a professional wrestler, he would become known as one of the most decorated and accomplished figures in the history of wrestling, as he competed across the country and in places such as Europe and Japan.

His name is Verne Gagne, and he was larger than life. He won the American Wrestling Association (AWA) Championship ten times between 1960 and 1981 and the AWA Tag Team Championship with Mad Dog Vachon in 1979. The nation watched as his matches sold out Madison Square Garden and he starred as a guest on Art Linkletter's talk show. He even met President Ford, Muhammad Ali, and Bob Hope.

Verne served as a wrestling promoter as well, training numerous wrestlers such as Ric Flair, the Iron Sheik, and Donna's brother, Greg Gagne. Greg formed the tag team "The High Flyers" with Jim Brunzell, and in 1977, they won the AWA World Tag Team Championship by defeating Blackjack Lanza and Bobby Duncum. Verne worked with other wrestlers too, such as Hulk Hogan and Andre the Giant. Donna remembers standing outside a wrestling ring with Andre when she noticed that her head barely touched his elbow. (She was 5'8" and Andre was 7'5"—with a size 24 shoe.) To others, Verne was the heavyweight champion of the world . . . but to Donna, he was the father who she knew and loved.

During the last six years of her father's life, Donna would serve as one of his primary caregivers. He was living with her sister and brother-in-law, so the thought was that Donna and her brother-in-law would alternate shifts taking care of him. Verne had Alzheimer's disease, so he had symptoms such as anxiety, memory loss, confusion, difficulty reasoning, and other cognitive impairments. Physically, Verne was in his eighties, but mentally, his mind would race back to years gone by. He would ask questions like, "Where's Mom?" even though she had died when he was just twelve years old.

When Donna and her siblings were growing up, their dad would get creative with how he helped raise them. For example, when he and his wife took the kids out west to go skiing, he had to think of ways to keep track of them on the slopes. So he would do things like yodel from the chairlift—that way, they could yodel back to let him know where they were skiing and that they were okay.

Now it was Donna's turn to get creative when taking care of him. Alzheimer's disease would certainly make that a challenge, so she learned to use things in everyday life to help him as the loved one with Alzheimer's and her as a dedicated caregiver.

Verne was raised on a farm with cows and chickens. Years later when he and his wife were raising their children, they had everything from dogs and cats to horses, parakeets, and a sheep named "Willie," so Donna knew that her dad had a love of animals that had spanned decades. (One of the parakeets would even ride around on her dad's head!) She learned that with Alzheimer's, it's common for people to have short-term memory loss, so she reasoned that his love of pets from years prior could still be relevant years later. This is where her lovable dachshund Pete came into play. If Verne objected to getting in the car when Donna wanted to run errands with him, she would say, "But, Dad, Pete's already in the car waiting for you, and he's ready to go!" Verne's demeanor would then soften as he gladly got into the car to "ride with Pete." The little dachshund was also helpful if Donna wanted her dad to go to sleep for the night. She would say, "Okay, Dad, it's time to go to bed."

He might reply by saying, "I'm not tired!"

And she would respond, "But Pete's tired, and he's waiting for you." Verne would then appear less anxious and head for bed.

Music was incredibly helpful as well. Wanting her dad to get some exercise so he could sleep through the night, Donna would play music for him. Not just any kind of music, as she knew that the salient stimulus of his favorite tunes would have the greatest effect by providing meaning for him. With that in mind, she would play either polka or country music as they danced or sang together in the home or outside on the deck.

As a caregiver of someone with Alzheimer's disease, Donna learned to adapt to different circumstances and tried to "go with the flow." She couldn't change or control the negative aspects of the disease, but she could at least get creative in how she responded to them. Having her dad run errands with her was great exercise for him, but there were obstacles for her. Each time they went to Target, it was almost as if it was the first time for him—he would gaze in awe at the bright lights and shiny merchandise. As they made their way up and down the aisles, he would put large items that they didn't need in the cart. Knowing from past experience that this would happen, Donna purposely let him walk ahead of her so that she could put the items back on the shelves without him knowing it. During one trip in particular, Verne stopped in front of a wall of candy and said with outstretched arms, "Wait a minute! Isn't this beautiful?!" Donna smiled and agreed with him. As he continued to admire the colorful candy, he said, "And you know what? It's good for ya!" This was especially touching because for years, Verne was a huge advocate of vitamins and eating healthy. As the caregiver, Donna knew that she needed to meet his needs, but in that moment, as his daughter, she also wanted to acknowledge his wants. Needless to say, she smiled on the inside as they drove home and her dad enjoyed his new candy.

Among the challenges and uncertainties of Alzheimer's disease, the ability to laugh was paramount. During one of her stays with Verne, Donna played a wrestling video for them to enjoy together. She had known for years that when her dad watched any type of athletics, he would get really into it, so it came as no surprise when he began to move toward the TV. As he did so, he started to say things like, "Look at that idiot! He can't wrestle!" and "Come on, buddy—get up!"

Donna just sat back and thought to herself, "I'll wait until this is over before I tell him who's wrestling." When the match was done, she said to him, "Guess who that was."

He replied, "Who? He was terrible!"

Donna responded, "Dad, that was you!" While she couldn't take away the stressors of the disease, the good-natured laughter that day could at least provide some comic relief and a great story for years to come.

Near the end of his life, hospice care workers brought a hospital bed into the home for Verne. The railings on both sides of it were intended to protect him, but his mind went back into wrestling mode, thinking he was back in the ring. Imagine Donna's surprise when he tried to crawl over them or "go over the top rope"—a line he had made famous decades earlier.

Aging with Alzheimer's disease was an incredibly ominous journey as Verne's body stayed strong, but his mind became more and more compromised. When asked what she learned through her experience of working so closely with the disease, Donna said to try not to take it personally. While there can be an immense amount of compassion fatigue and emotional labor that accompany Alzheimer's disease, it's important for caregivers to remember that changes in a loved one's behavior are due to the disease, not conscious decisions on their part that reflect how they feel about you.

Verne passed away in 2015. At the funeral, his longtime friend and pro-wrestling announcer "Mean" Gene Okerlund gave one of the eulogies. As he stood in front of the packed church, Gene grabbed the microphone and said with his commanding voice, "I want to do this one last time . . . Ladiessssss and gentlemen . . . Let me introduce to you the Heavyweight Champion of the Worrrrld . . . Vernnnnnne Gagneeeee!" The sanctuary erupted in applause as fans, family, and friends began to stand side-by-side in honor of Verne, including Donna, his loving daughter and devoted caregiver.

VERNE GAGNE

Verne Gagne

Mystery Illness

When Jean Abbott was twelve months old, her parents noticed that she had trouble sitting up and learning how to walk. Their family doctor initially thought that these were problems she would outgrow, but by the time she was three, things had gotten worse. It was then that her parents sought out one of the best neurologists in the country. By the time Jean was nearly four, she was diagnosed as having spastic diplegia, which is now deemed to be a type of cerebral palsy. Her family had finally gotten their answer. Now they could move forward and get Jean the help she needed. The medical world can be mysterious, though, consisting of unknowns and symptoms that can be deceiving.

As part of her treatment plan, Jean would take muscle relaxers and different medications. Her family sought the advice of a physiatrist, a highly trained medical professional who focuses on whole-body treatment for the musculoskeletal system and pain-causing disorders. She would also see a physical therapist and receive exercises that she could do to improve her muscular stiffness, unsteady movements, and compromised sense of balance.

When Jean was in first grade, she began wearing braces on her legs at night with the hope that her legs would stretch as she slept. She was also given general anesthesia for surgery where a "shot block" was given to her groin area as a way to keep her knees from knocking. She would go on to have this done three or four more times—otherwise, her knees would turn in and hit each other as she tried to walk. Over time, the shots stopped working, so when she was twelve years old, she underwent another surgery. By detaching muscles from her hips and then reattaching them in a way that helped her walk without tripping herself, doctors modified her gate such that she was less apt to fall. Some of the muscles were also shortened.

From a young age, Jean knew she was different, but she was raised to believe that her disability didn't need to define her or stop her from doing most of the things she wanted to do. She drew strength from her sense of faith as well, believing that her physical constraints didn't need to limit her ability to be happy. Yes, she had limited mobility with her legs and a tightness that folded her left arm up against her side, but rather than concentrate on what she couldn't do, *she focused on the things that she could do.*

One of the most puzzling characteristics of her condition was that she fared better in the morning. She could still do her chores, walk easily, or ride a bike at that time. Given these enhanced capabilities, she learned to schedule things in the morning. Or, if she had something fun lined up that evening, she wouldn't do as much physical activity during the day, thereby saving her energy for the event. It also helped if she took a nap before she participated in activities later in the day. Without such measures, it became almost impossible to do things such as homework in the evenings because it would become incredibly difficult to even hold a pen. This lack of dexterity was due to a tightening of the muscles. Knowing that mornings seemed to work best, her parents enrolled her in activities like ceramics classes where she could paint and be social early in the day.

A lot of her core friends are still in her life to this day. Some other kids from her childhood were outright mean. In junior high, she was teased for "walking funny"—not just behind her back but when she could actually hear the bullies. While their words stung, they also confirmed her desire to press on and show the world that she has more to offer than meets the eye.

When it came time to leave for college, a mobility scooter was ordered to assist her in navigating the campus between studying for tests, writing papers, and meeting the homework deadlines along the way. Stress and sleep had the biggest impacts on her ability to function, and she needed to be mindful of this reality as she experienced life on her own. The dorm where Jean stayed didn't have air conditioning, so often, her window was open as she tried to sleep. The tradeoff was the blaring sounds of the trains going by every hour, on the hour. The continued lack of sleep and the added stress of it all led her to use her mobility scooter in the mornings too, as she had now also lost her ability to walk early in the day.

During Jean's sophomore year, a guy named Steve transferred to her school. He was the roommate of her friend's boyfriend, and over the next couple of years, they became good friends. They began to date and were married when she was twenty-four years old.

When Jean was in her late twenties, a medical device was planted under the skin of her abdomen along with tubing that went up her spine. The device was called an Intrathecal Baclofen Pump. It was about the size of a hockey puck, and its purpose was to supply her with muscle relaxers. By that time, she had two children under the age of three, and her symptoms appeared to be getting worse from increased stress and a lack of sleep. Her new neurologist had recommended the pump because in addition to taking care of her small children, Jean was working part-time outside the home and helping run her household. As her condition got worse, the physician kept raising the dose of the muscle relaxers until it got so high that Jean lost all of her muscle spasticity. Muscle spasticity is needed to hold yourself up and walk. Seeing that she continued to get worse, her physician would use a needle to inject more of the muscle relaxers into the pump, thinking they would help. Jean's condition had deteriorated to a point where she couldn't roll herself over in bed or even sit in a chair anymore without being propped up by pillows.

Jean was overmedicated, anxious, and depressed. She quit her job, feeling like she had lost everything that she had worked so hard for since she was a child. The muscle relaxers that were supposed to be helping her were actually hurting her, but the problem was hidden in plain sight as the dosage was increased again and again. The increased dosage also compromised her emotional and mental health.

Feeling like a shell of her former self, Jean began to see a counselor. Thinking that her husband and kids would be better off without her, she debated whether she should look into a nursing home. Steve worked second shift, so their five-year-old daughter would make peanut butter and jelly sandwiches so that she and Jean could have "picnic" dinners in Jean's bedroom before she helped her mom get into bed for the night. In the morning, Steve would help Jean get in and out of the shower. As a wife and parent, Jean wanted to be a caregiver, but her family was taking care of her.

Jean's mom and Steve began to question what the doctor was doing with the muscle relaxers, so Jean started to see someone new. The new physician agreed that she was overmedicated, so she began to reduce the dosage of Jean's muscle relaxers. She also thought that something appeared to be odd with the diagnosis because the prior physician had noted in the file that Jean's condition was degenerative and had given her a new diagnosis without even telling Jean. By reducing the dosage, Jean could now function again, but there were still challenges, so she continued to ask others for help with her limited mobility. While the current doctor was able to run the clinic for the muscle relaxer pump, Jean was referred to a neurologist for a formal review of her diagnosis in order to see if anything should be changed.

Jean's brother brought her to the appointment with the new neurologist because she wasn't able to drive to and walk into the hospital by herself. Her husband, Steve, met them there. During the appointment, Steve happened to mention that it seemed like someone pressed a reset button when Jean took a nap or after she got a good night's sleep because then she could walk again. The neurologist's face began to light up as she quickly suggested that she didn't think Jean had cerebral palsy. She instead theorized that it was a rare movement disorder called Dopa-Responsive Dystonia (DRD). If that was the case, Jean could simply get on the correct medication and walk without needing help from anyone. Jean was skeptical because, at the age of thirty-three, she had endured decades of surgeries, medications, exercises, physical therapy, leg braces, and the Intrathecal Baclofen Pump, so how was one little pill supposed to solve everything? She had already accepted her condition and didn't need what appeared to be a false sense of hope.

During the car ride home, Steve expressed how he thought she should at least give the pill a try, knowing that she wouldn't have anything to lose. Initially, Jean wasn't even going to get the prescription filled, but she did so to humor him, more or less. It was Good Friday, and she took her first pill that same day. Later that evening, she went on to enjoy a glass of wine with dinner. When it was time to leave the restaurant, her husband approached her chair as usual, with the thought of helping her out of it. When she took his arm, she stood with ease. Instead of him having to half-carry her to the car, she held his hand and walked by his side. While this was great, she assumed that it was because the wine had helped relax her muscles.

When they got home, Jean got a good night's sleep, so the next day, when she was able to shower by herself, she chalked it up to all the sleep she had gotten the night before. The day after that was Easter Sunday. Their church was having an Easter egg hunt, so she and her husband stood in the church parking lot waiting for the festivities to begin. He let go of her and said he needed to go use the restroom. Knowing that she normally needed to secure her footing by relying on him, this seemed out of character. She would later learn that he did so because he believed that the medicine was working and that she *could literally and figuratively stand on her own*. Initially, Jean wasn't sure what to think, as she questioned how she could make her way to the church without falling. It was then that a sense of calm washed over her, as she realized that the *pills were working* and that the only way of life she had ever known was about to change forever. For years, she had believed that her condition could serve the greater good, and now she knew why. Rather than feel bitter about the surgeries, leg braces, hurtful jabs of peers, and doses of medications that she had never needed, she chose to view the decades of being misdiagnosed as a gift— not just for her, but for others—as positivity became her purpose.

Jean would learn that dopamine is made while people sleep. When the body doesn't produce enough of it, a person can have problems with movement. With the gift of hindsight, it makes sense that her ability to walk would be better in the morning or after she had taken a nap. Stress can also compromise the production of dopamine, and that's why the trains that plowed past her open dorm room window at college, which had kept her from sleeping well, had contributed to her inability to walk the next day. It also makes sense that the stress of being a new mom with two children under the age of three who was also responsible for the maintenance of a home and working part-time would fuel her condition. The new medication served as a synthetic form of dopamine, thereby giving her the quality of life that she could have had years earlier. She still has to get plenty of sleep and to remain as stress-free as possible. Otherwise, she can suffer from incredibly sore muscles, cramps, tremors in her hands, and issues with her sense of balance.

At the time of her epiphany that Easter Sunday, Jean's children were seven and five. A week or so after her diagnosis, she was home with just her five-year-old daughter, when it was time to get the mail. After telling her daughter where she was going, Jean stood in the garage and debated whether she should use her mobility scooter to get to the mailbox or take the chance and walk there. Not wanting to squander her amazing new gift, she decided to try walking there herself. It had been windy the last couple of days, and after she got the mail, she noticed a piece of paper in her yard, presumably from their recycling bin. She decided to take the chance of stepping onto the uneven ground to pick it up. It was then that she noticed another piece of paper a little bit farther away, so she made her way there too . . . and then onto the next one and the next. It took her a while, but she was able to get all the scattered pieces of paper herself. As she got back into the house, she could see that her daughter was standing by the window crying, so she asked her if she was scared. Through tears, her daughter said, "No, I'm just so happy that you can walk."

Jean's uplifting story of positivity and emotional grit has now inspired people around the world. By sharing her experience with others, Jean offers them the chance to draw strength from it as well. People realize that it is possible to find refuge in what you have rather than harbor resentment toward what you don't. While she can never get back the years when her health was compromised and her condition was misdiagnosed, Jean's story shows that it is possible to view life through a lens of gratitude every step of the way.

Battling Addiction

When my friend Nancy was raising her two sons, she served as one of their school's homeroom mothers and as a crossing guard. She was also a homemaker and Sunday-school teacher who prided herself on caring for her sons in a supportive environment with unconditional love. The best of intentions can only go so far, though, when competing with the throes of addiction.

Roughly at the age of fifteen, her son Casey began to use drugs. No single event brought this to her attention—rather, a series of things such as bad behavior and his desire to skip school did. She recalls that she was initially in complete denial because his older brother was a rule follower and had been easy to raise. By connecting the dots of Casey's life, red flags began to emerge, along with a mother's love that desired to save him. She knew that there were consequences for breaking the law, so she wasn't trying to make excuses for him, but she also wished that more people could see addiction as a complex disease that affects the brain rather than just a choice made by the individual.

The coming years would bring shady friends, jail, and even prison into Casey's life. With the help of the police, Casey's girlfriend, and parole officers, Nancy learned where the "haunts" were around town where people would buy and sell drugs. They lived in Grand Forks, North Dakota, so on some cold winter nights, she would leave home in her robe and pajamas to drive around looking for him in weather that was well below zero. After he didn't come home one night, he walked in the door the next day just as she was about to call the police to report him missing. She later found out that he had been held captive by drug dealers who were convinced that he was withholding information from them. Unable to answer their questions, he had spent the night in the trunk of their car as they drove around Grand Forks threatening him.

The dangers and uncertainties of addiction were more than Nancy could bear. While there were times when she could find her son, other nights, she would drive home, wondering if he would do the same. One time when he was missing, she sat down to write his obituary. As she did so, she decided that she would publicly disclose the dangers of addiction rather than succumb to them privately. She would later learn that her son was still living, but feelings of ambiguous grief began to overtake her as the boy she once knew was disappearing before her eyes and trouble continued to ensue. One day, she actually drove to a known drug house, opened the door unannounced, grabbed her son by the shirt, and pulled him out to safety.

As hard as it was for her and her husband to go through this excruciating experience as parents, it was even more difficult for Casey as the addict. One night, he sat on the edge of their bed and woke up Nancy, saying through tears that he didn't want to be the black sheep of the family anymore. When she told him that he wasn't and that he was deeply loved, he responded by calling out the fact that all of his cousins and friends had graduated from high school and gone to college, whereas he had been in treatment at the age of eighteen and had turned twenty-one in jail. Yes, the drugs were enticing, but the reality of his condition was catching up with him. He went on to earn his GED in a treatment center as he fought against the addiction.

Addiction can affect siblings as well, through feelings of frustration, misunderstanding, and anger. For example, they may wonder why Mom and Dad are giving so much attention to the sibling with the addiction when they themselves have worked hard, gotten good grades, and gone to college. Observing these feelings firsthand, Nancy explained to her older son that this wasn't a matter of *want* on her part but a matter of *need* for Casey. She also explained that she loved them both very much—and that it was possible to hate the disease without hating the person. Knowing that her older son isn't alone in his thoughts, Nancy would like to make a difference by helping the siblings of addicts feel acknowledged, heard, and supported.

Casey was in seven different drug-treatment facilities, usually for twenty-eight days each. These visits were followed by time at a sober house for thirty days. The most recent sober house Casey lived at is in South Carolina. It has businesses that help sustain it, including a moving company, a landscaping business, and a Christmas tree sales company. People new to the house do things such as serve meals, clean toilets, and do dishes. Each day starts at 7:00 a.m. and goes until 10:00 p.m., but the longer someone is there, the more privileges they can earn. During Casey's first year at the sober house, he began to speak more clearly and have a more positive view of the world. After his two-and-a-half-year stay, he had completed the program, stayed sober, and started to earn an associate's degree in computer science.

When asked how she got through this painful time, Nancy credits her own parents. She speaks of their unwavering love and the comfort that came from knowing they were by her side. By doing the same for her boys, she could stay strong for Casey, even when drugs continued to fail him. Knowing that there may be challenges in the years that lie ahead, her heart is filled with gratitude for how far they have come because she and her family were able to face their fears and learn from them.

Her ongoing desire is to help others do the same by sharing messages of hope through their story of emotional grit.

The Selfless Power of Perspective

When I worked with Tracy Murray, she and her husband, Brad, knew that they wanted to adopt a child. As part of the incredibly detailed paperwork for an adoption agency, they individually answered deeply personal questions about themselves, and as a couple, they answered questions about the way they would raise a child. They also participated in a three-day adoption class and had several home studies by a social worker. After that, they were allowed to put their bio in the "waiting families' book" for biological parents to read when considering the different couples who wanted to adopt.

After waiting for nearly a year, they were notified by another couple in the book about a three-month-old baby girl with Turner syndrome who was waiting to be adopted. Turner syndrome is a genetic disorder that affects females when one of the X chromosomes is missing in part or in full. It can cause a number of medical and developmental problems such as a shortness in stature, infertility, and heart defects.

Wanting to provide the baby girl with a loving home, Tracy and her husband followed the necessary steps and sent their profile to her biological parents for consideration. The girl's biological parents agreed that they would be a good fit for their daughter and wanted to move forward with the adoption.

Three weeks later, Tracy and Brad packed a car full of supplies such as toys, diapers, clothes, and a crib—and were on their way to Las Vegas to pick up the baby girl.

After a year of waiting to be chosen, along with the additional paperwork in Las Vegas, the baby girl was placed in their arms. She was now theirs, and they named her Rhiana Jade. (Jade was their favorite gemstone because its name means "a stone that protects and supports a loving heart," and that's exactly what they intended to do.)

Turner syndrome has its challenges. Tracy knew that Rhiana would need growth hormone shots and treatments for her congenital heart defect, including echocardiograms and lots of doctor appointments. She also knew that certain subjects at school would be hard for her, including geometry, because Turner syndrome can affect visual-spatial concepts. There was also a strong likelihood that Rhiana would have moments of doubt where she would wonder, "Why can't I be normal?"

How did Tracy know these things? She, too, has Turner syndrome, so she has firsthand knowledge of the uncertainties, fear, and self-doubt associated with it. However, her desire to embrace the challenges of the syndrome with Rhiana was greater than her willingness to be intimidated by them. After all, the wisdom that time had afforded her could now serve as a gift for the baby girl she had just met and for strangers who would later learn about their story of emotional grit.

Tracy, Brad, and Rhiana Murray

Beating the Odds

When Brent Harapat and two of his friends wanted to bet on the Super Bowl, they decided to have a guys' trip to Las Vegas. Wanting his family to have a nice weekend as well, Brent flew his mother-in-law to the Twin Cities so she could spend time with his wife and their twenty-two-month-old daughter. He would soon learn that the best-laid plans can go astray when life has other plans for you.

While in Vegas, Brent and his friends kept things low-key while placing their bets and playing poker. They didn't party hard, so when Brent woke up around 3:00 a.m. the morning of the game, he was surprised to be feeling sick. It was mostly the chills, so he fell back asleep, assuming it was the flu. When he woke up later that morning, he felt a bit better, so he joined the other guys for breakfast. As the day progressed, he felt more and more fatigued, so he looked into changing flights. The change fee was expensive, so he kept his red-eye flight and somehow managed to drive home from the airport. He barely remembers making the drive, but he knows that his head felt feverish while his hands felt cold.

Noting that his coloring was different than usual and that he appeared to have labored breathing, Brent's wife suggested that they go to urgent care to figure out what was wrong. Within minutes of getting there, he was placed on a table so that his vital signs could be taken. It was then that things got even more complicated because he began to turn blue. The medical team rushed him to the emergency room where more tests could be run; then Brent was asked for his permission to be intubated. At some point, he had a seizure, so his wife was hurried out of the room. Later, he was told they didn't think he would make it through the night.

Nearly three weeks later, Brent woke up with shriveled fingers that had turned black. The symptoms he had felt during the Vegas trip weren't those of the flu, as doctors discovered that he had pneumonia that went septic. The poisoning of his blood began to cause a massive shutdown of his organs. Days of heavy dialysis and other procedures had to be done to resume his bodily functions. In just the nick of time, he was stabilized. Through it all, Brent's body wanted to protect the internal organs, so it shunted blood from his extremities into his core. As a result, the negative impact was to his fingers.

At one point, Brent decided to get out of his hospital bed, presumably to use the restroom. In a drug-induced state, he crawled over the railing and crashed onto the floor, unable to get his footing. At first glance, he thought there was dirt on the floor and that it had gotten all over his ankles and feet. He would soon learn that the problem wasn't with the floor, it was that sepsis had also taken the use of his feet. They were blackened, just like his fingers and ankles. They were somewhat curled and almost looked mummified. He hadn't noticed this before because most of his body was covered while in the hospital bed.

Doctors would need to amputate most of his fingers first. He still has one left on his right hand, which is his dominant one, and two and a half on the left. His feet and the lower parts of his legs were more complicated in that they weren't yet *healthy enough* to amputate and reconfigure the area. (Yes, the extremities could technically be removed, but the residual limbs, including the sur-rounding tissues, needed to heal to a point where staples or stitches would actually stay in place and reduce the risk of infection.) Brent would need to wait several months before his body had healed enough for the remaining amputations to take place.

Once the final amputations were done, Brent needed time to heal again so that he could be fitted for his new prosthetic legs. The new prostheses did more than help him walk—they helped him regain his sense of freedom and the normalcy that he craved. Music played an important role as well because it helped carry him throughout the day and provided a sense of comfort through positive memories.

Rather than feel weighed down by his circumstance, Brent decided to lighten the mood through humor. When people would later ask him if he could still type, he would laugh and say, "For over eighteen years in corporate America, I typed with just two fingers, so now, I'm ahead of the game with three and a half!" He would also look at people and jokingly say, "You're number one!" as he held up his hand with its single finger. Even though he couldn't change his situation, laughter could help him embrace it. He certainly credits his supportive family as well.

When facing new challenges, Brent asks himself to this day, "How bad do you want it?" If it's something that is important to him, he'll either try to do it with the two and a half fingers on his non-dominant hand or get creative. For example, if he needs to carry his keys, lunch, and laptop, he'll do so in a backpack. Or if he needs to sign something, he'll use an adaptive pen (i.e., a pen that fits onto the end of a finger, almost like a thimble). He also has dress shirts with little pieces of Velcro hidden in plain sight where there would normally be buttons.

He can no longer perform certain tasks, so Brent keeps things in perspective by reminding himself that even when he was able-bodied, there were things he couldn't do—not as a way of dwelling on weakness but as a reality of being human.

While the bets in Vegas were placed on the Super Bowl, mine is on Brent. Knowing that the cards were stacked against him, he stayed true to his instincts and resisted the temptation to fold, showing that it's possible to play the house and win.

Grit at Ground Zero

In the early hours of September 11, 2001, Paul Falla had just finished a twenty-four-hour shift as an FDNY firefighter with

Engine 83 in the Bronx. As a junior member of his company, he was waiting for someone from another firehouse to replace him. It was then that alarms began to sound, so he had to board a fire rig instead, along with other members of his company, a fire captain who was covering for the day, and their chauffeur. Having heard that a plane hit the North Tower of the World Trade Center, they thought that was where they were supposed to report. They never dreamed that the crash was on purpose, so their day was about to change as initial assumptions of a tragic accident would soon become viewed as an act of war.

As they were heading down FDR Drive, someone on the rig looked at their ticket to confirm where they were supposed to go. It was then that they realized it must have initially been misread because they were driving in the wrong direction. They were supposed to be reporting to a staging area in Harlem where they could join five or six other FDNY companies and await further commands. After turning around near 23rd street, they drove to the staging area, where they were told to get back on their rig because they, along with the other companies, were heading to the World Trade Center.

During the ride to what would later be called "Ground Zero," Paul and the other members of his company learned that a second plane had hit the South Tower. Among feelings of ambiguity, there was now suspicion as to what had just happened. After the rig was parked, they grabbed "roll-ups" (i.e., fifty-foot lengths of 2.5" hose lines), their helmets and gloves, a self-contained breathing apparatus (SCBA), and other gear before making their way by foot to the World Trade Center. There was a lot of chaos, smoke, and debris, so initially, they didn't realize that the South Tower had already fallen, as it was hard to see. They were close enough to the North Tower to watch as it began to fall before their very eyes. The menacing noise was that of a loud "swishing sound" paired with a series of deafening booms. As the debris began to fly towards them with incredible speed, the captain told them to "drop everything and run," which they did while wearing one-hundred-plus pounds of gear.

It was hard to see and even harder to breathe. The world around them would alternate between total blackout and complete whiteout as smoke, dust, reams of paper, and a thick, dense rolling cloud of debris began to pummel the streets with purpose. There were no solid desks, office chairs, or computers, just hard-packed residuals and the remains of those who used them—including the outstretched hand of a woman with freshly painted nails sticking out of the debris.

At the age of thirty-one, this was Paul's second year on the job. He was nervous and scared because he and his company weren't able to use their SCBAs, so it was especially hard to breathe. As he and the other members of his company began to regroup, they could see cars on fire, people running for their lives, and fellow first responders trying to help with little-to-no direction. A recall had taken place that day, calling firemen of the FDNY back to their firehouses for further orders. Regardless of where they were, they needed to drop what they were doing and report for duty. There was no rulebook as something of this magnitude was unprecedented.

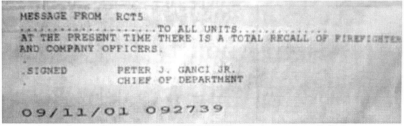

Total recall notice for FDNY firefighters on 9/11

Things got eerily quiet, but then Paul heard transmissions from officers and a captain who were looking for firemen by name, which isn't the normal protocol. They were trying to create some semblance of order as chaos ensued and people became separated. Later, there would be stories describing how women's high-heeled shoes had been strewn in the street because it was easier to take them off to run. Cars were left at train stations as their owners weren't able to retrieve them—because they had passed away.

Paul and his company worked until about one the next morning without food or water, breathing in contaminated air the entire time. They suffered from complete exhaustion as members of the Red Cross periodically wiped soot from their eyes. At 2:00 or 3:00 a.m., they made their way back to their firehouse. As the rig approached the station, they could see other members of the firehouse waiting for them in the street. Not knowing if Paul and his company were dead or alive, the others greeted them by street light with hugs and tears. The surprising reunion was especially emotional given the fact that Paul's rig had initially been heading straight to the World Trade Center the day before. Had they not incurred the twenty to twenty-five-minute delay before driving to the staging area in Harlem, they, along with the other engine companies that joined them, likely would have been in the first tower as it collapsed.

Having worked for forty-plus hours over two shifts, Paul took a shower and fell asleep in one of the firehouse chairs. Over the next couple of days, he would head back to Ground Zero on a city bus with other firemen and police escorts. As they did so, they prepared themselves to conduct search-and-rescue efforts before focusing on recovery, as they knew most potential survivors wouldn't be able to survive without water for more than three days.

The FDNY created two-week shifts in which members were deployed for twelve-hour days so that they could conduct "bucket brigades" (i.e., use handheld buckets to remove debris, passing each bucket onto the next person). The lines consisted mostly of firemen from multiple companies and police officers. Of the nearly 3,000 victims who perished at the site of the World Trade Center due to the terrorist attacks of 9/11, 403 of them were first responders: 343 New York City firemen, 23 NYPD officers, and 37 police officers from the Port Authority of New York and New Jersey. It was very likely that Paul and his crew would find some of their own in the rubble. Weeks into their efforts, Paul would learn that the remains of a firefighter from his firehouse were found among the ruins at Ground Zero. A battalion chief had been notified as well before watching the remains being pulled from the debris. The chief and Paul were two of the people who helped carry him. By profession, they were serving a fellow firefighter, but by blood, the battalion chief was grieving the loss of a loved one, as the deceased firefighter was also his son.

On 9/11, hospitals braced themselves for an onslaught of injured people that would never come. That's because people either made it out and away from the buildings in time or went down with them. With few bodies recovered or confirmed dead, families held memorial services with the hopes that their loved ones were still living. For one solid year, Paul would attend multiple memorial services a day with members of his firehouse. At times, he would go on his own. Attending those services was important because as first responders, Paul and his crew wanted to show respect for people who were missing or who died in the line of duty, even if they had never known them. Due to the sheer number of services, at times, they had to choose which ones to attend because one might be in New Jersey at the same time as another on Long Island. Such memorial services would normally feature large groups of people playing bagpipes and drums, but due to the high volume of services, sometimes they had to split into smaller groups. The cadence of their hauntingly beautiful sounds served as a reminder that another hero was being laid to rest. The services and music promoted closure, but such feelings were cut short if the remains of the missing person were found months later, so a second service would be held in that person's honor.

Paul was at Ground Zero in the early hours of December 25, 2001. After working for a period of time, he began to wander the cold, dark streets. They were busy, but he felt very much alone. Then he spotted St. Paul's Chapel, part of the Parish of Trinity Church Wall Street. Built in 1766, it sits across from the World Trade Center site, yet it suffered no physical damage. Now known as the "Chapel that Stood," on 9/11 and the days that followed, it embraced thousands of exhausted and weary rescue and recovery workers such as police officers, port authority workers, firemen, sanitation crews, and more. However, at roughly 4:00 a.m. that Christmas morning, it was just Paul and four to five strangers. He was the only one wearing "bunker gear" (e.g., a fire coat, fire pants, and boots) as he entered the chapel and kneeled. Reflecting on the shock and disbelief of everything he had seen over the last four months—the carnage among the billowing smoke, tangled steel, ruins, and debris—he knew how he was feeling, but he questioned, "What does this all mean? What am I doing here?" He then began to pray as his desire to serve others strengthened his resolve.

This selfless mindset can be attributed to other first responders as well. When Paul first wanted to become a firefighter in 1992, he couldn't do so for *seven years* because there was a waitlist of people wanting to serve—people who were willing to put the lives of others ahead of their own—people who persevered, just like Paul, and exemplified the power and strength of emotional grit.

Closing

◆ ◆ ◆

It has been said that necessity breeds ambition, and while it's easy to assume the grass is greener on the other side, it's empowering to know that we can water our own. Life can *test* us, but it can also *teach* us by providing opportunities for patience, perseverance, and grit. With time and experience comes the wisdom of knowing when to roll with the punches and when to stand your ground. Identifying your source of motivation can provide clarity because it offers an incentive to continue when life gets tough. I know I've made pain my purpose because my desire to give others a sense of hope is greater than my willingness to extinguish my own. I can "justify" my brain-tumor scare because so many positive things have come out of it. While there are no guarantees that the tumor won't someday return, I've chosen to focus on what I *know* rather than what I could *fear*.

So, what's your "greater than"? Is it that your desire to do something is greater than your fear of it? This doesn't mean that you can't be afraid, it just means that you're going to persevere anyway. Your journey may be down a road less traveled, but the path you take can be filled with things that lower stress along the way. The best things in life are free. That is the power and strength of emotional grit.

About the Author

• • •

Jennifer Fernjack is an author and keynote speaker. She has shared her message of "emotional grit" at places such as the Mayo Clinic, HealthPartners Neuroscience Center, the University of Minnesota Duluth, Gilda's Club, and more. Raised in Cloquet, Minnesota, she currently resides in Spring Park, Minnesota. She has a BA degree from the University of Minnesota Duluth and an MBA from the University of St. Thomas. Jennifer's personal story of emotional grit stems from a health scare where she learned that the best things in life are free.

She can be reached at Jenniferfernjack.com or 952-451-5925.

Jfernjack@
yahoo.com